Patricia Mignon Hinds, *Editor*   *Text by* Audrey Edwards

ESSE

Harry N. Abrams, Inc., *Publishers*

Introduction *by* Susan L. Taylor *Foreword by* Maya Angelou

25 Years Celebrating Black Women

For Harry N. Abrams, Inc.:
Editor: Ruth A. Peltason
Designers: Judith Michael and Beth Tondreau

For *Essence:*
Additional writing by
Utrice Leid
Deborah Gregory
Pamela Johnson
Art Consultant: Charles Dixon III

Captions for pages 1–7:
Norma Jean Darden, now one of New York's popular caterers, was
a featured model in the earliest issues of *Essence*. May 1970,
Photo, Richard Noble; Halle Berry, actress known for her versatility
and beauty, in the desert of New Mexico for an *Essence* shoot.
January 1992, Photo, Kip Meyer; Oprah Winfrey, the multi-Emmy
Award-winner, is at the helm of a powerful entertainment
enterprise. May 1995, Photo, Matthew Jordan Smith; Angela Davis.
January 1995, Photo, Matthew Jordan Smith; Carol Moseley-Braun
assumed a coveted position of power as the first Black woman
elected to the U.S. Senate. October 1992, Photo, Ruven Afanador;
Actress Alva Rogers appeared in the film *Daughters of the Dust*.
January 1993, Photo, Matthew Jordan Smith; A cultural twist.
January 1994, Photo, John Peden

LIBRARY OF CONGRESS CATALOGING-IN-PUBLICATION DATA

Edwards, Audrey.
Essence: 25 years celebrating Black women/Patricia Mignon Hinds, editor;
foreword by Maya Angelou; introduction by Susan L. Taylor;
text by Audrey Edwards.
p.   cm.
ISBN 0-8109-3256-3
1. Essence.   2. Afro-American women.   I. Hinds, P. Mignon.
II. Title.
PN4900.E85E39   1995
305.48'96073'05—dc20   94-48521

Published in 1995 by Harry N. Abrams, Incorporated, New York
A Times Mirror Company

Printed and bound in Japan

Contents

Foreword

by Maya Angelou

I can't believe my good fortune, and I'm just so grateful, to be a Black woman. A Black American woman. I would be so jealous if I were anything else.

I remember saying this in a small group somewhere, and a white man actually said to me, "Now, come on, you know you wish you were a white man." I laughed so hard, I almost cried. I said, "Absolutely not! I cannot imagine having so much power and yet being incapable of using it in a positive way. I dare not even conjecture what it would do to my psyche, to know that the factors that created my supposedly privileged place in society are the very reasons I am prevented from using whatever power I have for good. It must be an awful burden to bear — to know that if I tried to use my power in a positive way, my people would laugh at me, scorn me, jeer me, and probably disown me. So no, I have no desire to trade places with a white man."

As a Black woman, I know where I have come from. I have nursed a nation of strangers. People I knew would grow up to threaten and maim and kill my own; I have nursed them. I have held together our greatest institutions, the family and the church, and kept the Black man at the top. I have come out of the fields of Alabama, out of the Mississippi Delta, out of the deserts of Texas. I have been creative, constantly taking chances — racehorse chances — to negotiate my path. I have used a number of ploys to erect my own bridges over boiling waters, laughing when I wasn't tickled and scratching when I didn't itch. And I am here — still here, despite the odds.

Being a woman is not about being born female; being born with certain genitalia will only make a person an old whatever-the-genitalia-dictates if the person lives long enough. To be a woman is to take responsibility for your actions and for the time you consume and the space you occupy. It is to strive for constancy in all things — to stretch, to grow, to be courageous enough to change course or change your mind as you discover new truths. It is about assuming the responsibility to find yourself within yourself, to find your own personal power source. To be a woman is to defy outright any idea that would put you in a trick bag, that would inhibit growth, that would bind and limit. To be a woman is to compel yourself to search out and embrace ideas that liberate, that make you bigger, finer, stronger, more courageous, more generous, more merciful. To be a woman is to work hard, to count on yourself, to owe nothing. It is to hold the reins of your life in your own hands.

Maya Angelou's masterful words resonate deep truths within us.
December 1992
Photo, Dwight Carter

While there are other groups of women who were pushed to the edge and jumped off or surrendered or gave up, and lots of other folks who have capitulated to the blows and slings and arrows of outrageous fortune, Black women have stood up strong every time. I don't know why; I can't explain why this is so. But I know that we have, and I know that we do. Perhaps we are made strong by struggle. It is in this sense that I believe my story is a Black woman's story, and my life the life of Black women.

I was raped when I was a girl, and was approached many times after that by people who were interested in me sexually, just sexually. At sixteen I had a baby, and at seventeen I took my baby and hit the road, grabbing any job that came my way so I could keep my baby on my hip. One might have been inclined to think, "Well, this makes me a woman." But really, I was just female.

My mother was the person who gave me my first inkling that I was a woman. I was about twenty-one years old and had gone to visit her in San Francisco. I was holding down two jobs at the time, still raising my child by myself, living on my own. Life was always tough—I was always close to the edge, barely hanging on—but I never would ask her for help, even though I knew she gladly would have given it.

We had had lunch and we walked down the hill together, and when we got to the bottom of the hill she turned to me and said very sweetly, "Baby, you know something? I think you're the greatest woman I've ever met." I looked at her, Vivian Baxter, this little five-foot-four woman dressed in a beautiful suit and wearing a wonderful fur and diamond earrings, and she said, "Yes, because you're very intelligent and you're very kind, and those two qualities are rarely found together. So you are a great woman." Then she said, "Give me a kiss." I kissed her, and she crossed the street and got into her yellow Pontiac. I crossed the street the other way and waited for the streetcar.

I got on the streetcar—I remember it so clearly, the time of day, the way the sun hit the seats—and I sat there and thought to myself, "Suppose she's right? Suppose I really am somebody? Suppose I really am a great woman?" I began to look at myself, to look at the things I was doing, the way I was living my life. I saw myself with these two jobs raising a child, being independent and kind, and I thought, "Well, maybe I am!"

It was a glorious, precious moment when this affirmation and self-realization came to me, so many years after my wonderful brother, Bailey—who is almost two years older than I and the closest my family has ever come to producing a genius—had told me that I was very smart. "All knowledge is spendable currency, depending on the market," I remember him saying to me when I was about ten years old, quoting from some book he had read. This one sentence had made such an impression on him that he wanted it to have meaning for me, too. And so, to please him—because I knew he loved me and would never lie to me, telling me I was smart if I really wasn't—I tried to learn everything. By then, Mama, my paternal grandmother, a very powerful woman who had raised me, had brought me to the realization that I was a single person, that I belonged to myself. That, however, did not inform me that I was a woman. It was Vivian Baxter, my mother, who freed me. She fixed me firmly in an understanding of womanhood. She anointed me a woman person.

No one owes this woman, Maya Angelou, anything. No one. And so I marvel at my good fortune and I am very, very grateful. I rejoice that people love me, and that I've reached age sixty-six feeling and looking pretty good, and am still out here doing things that have meaning for me. I believe in hard work, and I see evidence now of the work I've put in. But I know, as a Christian woman and religious person, that I have been saved and protected from some things that could have ended my life and ended it very badly. In the end, some chances I took served me very well; others did not. But nothing is owed me, and I take nothing for granted—not my life, not my gifts, not my talents, not love.

There is a fabulous Ethiopian song my friends taught me thirty years ago that was banned in Addis Ababa by Emperor Haile Selassie. The song's message is meant to make the listener very uncomfortable and fix a humbling thought in the mind, which is why I like it. It says: "Don't tell me how beautiful you are, or how rich you are, or what a high position you hold, or how pretty you are, or how wise. For if you do, you will make me take you to the edge of the world and show you where people far better off than you have tried to jump off." So I take nothing for granted—including the heady, wonderful privilege of being a Black woman. This is not a passive exercise; it requires work that at times can be very painful. Pain often accompanies privilege.

Built into the privilege of being a Black woman should be an ever-present consciousness that we have been, and still are, targeted for attack. This consciousness should inform our actions, our decisions, and our sense of who we are and what we are about. But we should be careful not to allow it to overwhelm or immobilize us. Rather than allowing my mind to be preoccupied with these negative forces, I direct my energy toward moving on, moving ahead. Instead, I am preoccupied with another program—inquiring about and discovering the world, the environment around me, and how I and my people fit into it and have interacted with it. I am preoccupied observing the truth of Einstein's theory of relativity—that there's no such thing as regression in life, only constant change.

In the past twenty-five years, we have witnessed, as Black women, enormous change, the greatest being an increased awareness and, in many instances, realization, of our power. It is, I believe, one of our most significant achievements. In block associations and neighborhood groups, in civic and religious groups, in sororities and political parties, in the corporate world and the public sector, in practically every sphere of influence, Black women are wielding real, actual power, and it is helping in concrete, measurable ways to improve the nature of our existence as a race of people. We can put a company out of business if we decide that it isn't treating our people right. We can make the difference in the outcomes of political elections. Our views help shape the formulation of governmental policies. Our voices are speaking for our people who live under the yoke of tyranny and oppression all over the world.

But though we gained a lot of power, we also have sustained enormous damage. Nowhere is this more evident than in what is happening to our families. Until about thirty years ago, it seemed we advanced and we pulled our people with us; we pulled our families with us. Like the turtle that carries its babies on its back, it was the way we Black women came through slavery and managed our affairs, somehow, through the hoax of Reconstruction, through the years of lynching, through the years of migrations and perpetual dislocations. Now it appears that the strings that had held us together have become untied and we're seeing the result—the children are running crazy in the streets.

The challenge before us as Black women is to reestablish family ties and to create family, bound by blood or not. This, I am convinced, is our mandate. This is how we save ourselves as a people.

The best place to start, of course, is at home, where all virtues and vices begin. By *home* I don't just mean the physical setting in which we live; I mean that which is harbored within the breast, within the heart of the individual. A tree with a simple root structure won't easily survive a strong wind, but a tree whose roots go deep into the soil and is firmly anchored stands a far better chance. So it is with us, by anchoring ourselves in a spirituality which we set out in a purposeful, deliberate way to discover. And once we discover it, and we define it, and we cherish it, we are free to spread it and share it with our beloveds, our family and friends, and even people who aren't in our immediate circle. This is when we are at our best.

But even when we are at our worst, at our lowest ebb, we cannot waste time bemoaning our state, and we certainly can't give anybody the delicious satisfaction of knowing they have knocked us down and kept us there. When we are knocked down, we must pick ourselves up as quickly as we can and get on with the business of saving our lives before life dribbles away. Sometimes we can get so low, feel so betrayed, that we begin to question our own worth and think that we don't deserve love. When this happens, we should recognize and acknowledge that we have been wounded, but we should learn also to cauterize our wounds, to sear them shut until we have the luxury of time and the strength of heart to revisit and unseal them for examination. Our spirit and soul can drain through our wounds, if we allow.

Black woman to Black woman, we should be careful of anything that threatens to separate us, for if we are separated, we will be undone as a race. This is why I pay no attention whatsoever to the silliness some people would encourage us to dwell upon. What does it matter, for example, if a woman wants to frizz her hair or straighten it, wear it natural or braid it, cut it all off or wear a wig? We can choose anything we think enhances our beauty. Any idea is at its best when it liberates. Freedom is the right to live the way we want, for, in the end, our lives are all we really have, and only we have the authority to deconstruct and reconstruct ourselves.

Black women for centuries have had to depend on other Black women to keep ourselves, our homes, our institutions and our communities together. With the conditions that loom before us as a people and the awesome challenges we face, it would be genocidal to break the bond of sisterhood. This is why I make a conscious effort to say to my sisterfriends that I love and cherish them, that my life is diminished without their presence and participation in it. I thank them for being in my corner. We try to find wonderful things to say to each other that we really mean — "I love seeing you." "You look great." "You're important to my eyes and ears." We give each other little gifts, or send cards, or call just to say hello. In short, my sisterfriends and I have resolved to hold on to and be there for each other, all the way. I have absolute faith that I could lean on any one of them and she wouldn't buckle; their expectations of me are exactly the same.

Shoring each other up, Black women do that as a rule. My sincerest wish is that we hold fast to it, and do it with love. We show what we believe by our own loving actions. Through love we teach. Through love we instruct. Through love we build up.

I think about us, women and girls, and I want to say something worth saying to a daughter, a friend, a mother, a sister—my self. And if I were to try, it might go like this:

Dear Us:

You were the rim of the world—its beginning. Primary. In the first shadow the new sun threw, you carried inside you all there was of startled and startling life. And you were there to do it when the things of the world needed words. Before you were named, you were already naming.

Hell's twins, slavery and silence, came later. Still you were like no other. Not because you suffered more or longer, but because of what you knew and did before, during and following that suffering. No one knew your weight until you left them to carry their own. But you knew. You said. "Excuse me, am I in the way?" knowing all the while that you were the way. You had this uncanny ability to shape an untenable reality, mold it, sing it, reduce it to its manageable, transforming essence, which is a knowing so deep it's like a secret. In your silence, enforced or chosen, lay not only eloquence but discourse so devastating that "civilization" could not risk engaging in it lest it lose the ground it stomped. All claims to prescience disintegrate when and where that discourse takes place. When you say, "no" or "yes" or "this and not that," change itself changes.

So the literature you live and write asks and gives no quarter. When you sculpt or paint, organize or refute, manage, teach, nourish, investigate, or love, you do not blink. Your gaze so lovingly unforgiving, stills, agitates, and stills again. Wild or serene, vulnerable or steel trap, you are touchstone by which all that is human can be measured. Porch or horizon, your sweep is grand.

You are what fashion tries to be—original and endlessly refreshing. Say what they like on Channel X, you are the news of the day. What doesn't love you has trivialized itself and must answer for that. And anybody who does not know your history doesn't know their own and must answer for that too.

You did all right, girl. Then at the first naming, and now at the renaming. You did all right. You took the hands of the children and danced with them. You defended men who could not defend you. You turned grandparents over on their sides to freshen sheets and white pillows. You made meals from leavings, and leaving you was never a real separation because nobody needed your face to remember you by. And all along the way you had the best of company—others, we others, just like you.

—Toni Morrison, "A Knowing So Deep," May 1985

Toni Morrison, author of
such wonderful works as
Song of Solomon, Sula,
and Beloved, *was the first*
African-American to win
the Nobel Prize for
literature, which she
received in 1993.
October 1983
Photo, Helen Marcus

I give you my hand in a moment of
sudden love and respect Essence magazine.
You are twenty-five years old, as old as
my twin sons. Having crossed twenty-five
years, I give you my eyes at this hour
of hunger breaking African children into a
fine rain of death;

I give you my heart because you understand
Black women are violets tied in little bunches.
Braids of hurt. The inevitable beat and color.
Whirlwinds of joy and rage. Equalizers of the evening
and morning star. Lovers of the anarchistic tongue.
Mothers in praise of pants and skirts, adjectives
and verbs, chapels and confessionals;

I give you my fist raised against this mad
vibration of death at the end of the twentieth century
where we are filthy with war,
where young veins bleed with lice,
where death cries out like morning birds.
But I have come to you out of Africa out of plantations
out of cities out of suburbs out of colonialism out of racism
out of sexism out of homophobia out of abuse out of alienation
out of my own legs running towards freedom and love
out of time marked by poets;

Now you and I both know as we move
behind the smell of our breathing,
toward the twenty-first century,
that we women must scrub skeletons back to life
exhale our funerals anoint
our feet in light as we genuflect peace and racial justice.
you and I must be reborn in stone in wind in water
kiss life on its two faces
make God finally break the habit of being man.

—Sonia Sanchez, July 1994

I like our style. I like the Black woman's strut. I like the fact that nothing gets us down for very long. I like the way we look; the way we talk; our ambition and our dreams. The young women today are using the best of the rest of us to wrestle through with their identities and responsibilities. I like our braids, our bleached and dyed hair, our blue contact lenses in our brown eyes. I like the way we aren't afraid of trying anything once and good things twice. I especially appreciate our sincerity. I like the fact that when we have questions, we aren't afraid to seek answers. And aren't afraid of the answers we find. I like our courage. In a world that continually assaults all that we are and that we stand for, I like the fact that we have stood and are standing for ourselves. I guess you could just say I like the essence of the Black woman. She's all right by me.

—Nikki Giovanni, July 1994

In the beginning . . .

by Susan L. Taylor

I'll never forget the first time I saw *Essence*. I was a new mother, living in the Bronx, dreaming dreams and planning for the future, getting ready to open the cosmetics company that I had been saving for and thinking about for some time. I had gone around the corner to pick up a newspaper at the candy store where I encountered a most beautiful bronze woman. She wore her hair natural, had full sensuous lips, and cheekbones carved almost up to her eyebrows. I couldn't take my eyes off her, and she just stared right back at me, with a silent bearing that spoke volumes. Confident and proud, she seemed to take in all the world and hurl back a challenge to a world that had for so long refused to see her. And this sister simply would not, could not, be ignored.

I was stunned. Not only because she was stunning, but because she appeared on the cover of a substantive, sophisticated new publication that boldly proclaimed her the essence of Black womanhood, or, deeper still, Black womanhood as the essence of something even greater. In either case, it was a truly revolutionary statement, a first. It was, in fact, the first issue of *Essence* magazine, and I'd almost swear it leaped into my arms. I bought the magazine, hurried home, and devoured it from cover to cover; then reread it slowly, savoring every page, every image of chocolate-mocha mix-caramel-café au lait, and licorice-black beauty flaunted, every unapologetic truth told, every righteous take on the issues from our perspective. There were articles on careers and relationships, on travel, on women in the struggle. There were fashion and beauty, food and culture, news and poetry. *Essence* was more than just another women's magazine. *Essence* was me.

And for me, as for most who saw that first issue, I'm sure it seemed as if *Essence* had simply appeared, like Aphrodite emerging from the sea, full grown in all her splendor and complexity. Few outside, of course, had any inkling of the struggle and sacrifice, the disappointments, the long hours, the labor that four young men had endured to give birth to their dream.

Essence Communications CEO and *Essence* magazine publisher, Edward Lewis, has been a guiding force since the magazine's conception. He says, "Not having had a child of my own, what I can point to is that I helped bring something

Barbara Cheeseboro, the commanding beauty from the first cover of Essence.
May 1970
Photo, Tomas

into the world from the beginning, and I've seen it go through early stages, adolescence, all the stages that one goes through, I think, in bringing up a child."

The parenting metaphor is apt. The worry, the concern, the turbulence behind the scenes at *Essence* during those early years is only hinted at on the magazine's masthead—in the listing of the officers and staff, which changed from issue to issue. But *Essence* was born in the struggle, of the struggle.

Those were turbulent times for us as a people. By mid-1968 Martin Luther King, Jr., had been assassinated, Malcolm was gone, young Black women and men were graduating from colleges in record numbers, White college students were questioning their parents about the disparities that exist between Black and White Americans. There was a great deal of unrest, not only on the nation's college campuses, but in its urban centers and inner cities as well. There were many who carried the banner of equality of opportunity into battle daily: to their jobs and into bold new business ventures, contending both with the outside forces arrayed against our forward progress and the disabling lack of consensus that sometimes wreaks havoc among us. Reluctantly, White America was beginning to recognize that Black people wanted into the system, and for a brief period in the late 1960s and early 1970s there seemed to be a new spirit of encouraging Black people to get into business. At the time, there was a lot of talk about creating a strong Black economic base through entrepreneurship.

"It was a very traumatic year for me," Essence Communications President Clarence O. Smith observes of 1968, the year the *Essence* founders first came together. "It started in April with Dr. King's assassination. In June of that year, my sister and her husband lost their lives in a train wreck, and Robert Kennedy was assassinated. I remember, particularly when Dr. King was killed, feeling guilty that I really hadn't been involved in the civil rights movement other than the way in which many middle-class Blacks were. I went to the March on Washington. But I really wasn't making a contribution. So I really felt I needed to make a change in my life—that I must do something with whatever talent I have to serve Black people better, so when my son, who was then a year old, would ask me what I was doing in those days, I wouldn't have to say I was making the insurance industry richer."

In 1968 Clarence was working for a major insurance company, angry and looking for a way out. "I began to realize that the life insurance companies were responsible for a lot of the deprivation and ghetto existence of African-Americans. They were taking money from people, giving them a very poor return on their money, and then taking this money and investing it in tracks of real estate, commercial buildings, and other kinds of property. And they were responsible for not picking up mortgage paper from Black banks. The insurance companies redlined Black areas, so Black banks were kept poor."

Beating the odds: Essence *founders with Gordon Parks, editorial director (seated front), left-right: Jonathan Blount, Clarence O. Smith, Ed Lewis, Cecil Hollingsworth. May 1970 Photo, Alfred Statler*

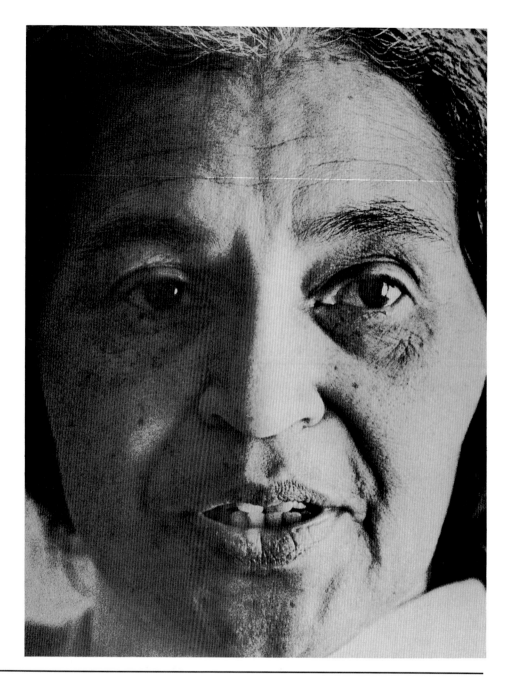

Civil rights activist Rosa Parks, a year after Detroit renamed its Twelfth Street in her honor.
May 1970
Photo, Gordon Parks

The anger and frustration felt by Clarence Smith was expressed in various ways by millions of Black people across the socio-economic spectrum of America. The burning of America's cities following the assassination of Dr. King, the birth of the Black Power movement, the rise of militant new voices like those of H. Rap Brown and Stokely Carmichael were the signs of the times. "White people were frightened," says Clarence, "and some decided that something should be done to try to assuage this feeling of hurt and rage that Black people had. And how do capitalists do that? Make everybody rich. Richard Nixon was running for the presidency and talking about Black capitalism and promoting the idea of minority small business investment companies getting started by the Chases and the Citibanks and the Morgans of the world. A lot of Black businesses got started back in 1968, 69 and 70. The climate was such, and it almost seemed as if corporate America was trying to apologize to Blacks for setting the climate in which Dr. King was killed. I mean, it was almost like they were saying, 'Stop burning down the cities and we'll behave ourselves better.'"

Russell Goings, a race man whom Ed Lewis calls the godfather of *Essence*, was an assistant vice president for Shearson, Hammill & Company, the Wall Street investment banking and brokerage firm that had recruited him in 1968 to open a branch office on 125th Street, which would eventually become First Harlem Securities Corporation. Part of his mission was to identify and develop business opportunities for Blacks. "In order to open a branch, Shearson needed to develop credibility," says Goings. "There was a suspicion and a fear among some in the community that Shearson was going to go in and rape 125th Street. So they needed some demonstration of Black people doing their own business."

Russ Goings and his wife, Mattie M. Goings, who was the community coordinator at Shearson, put together a list of up-and-coming young African-Americans in corporate America and invited them to a series of meetings entitled "So You Wanna Be in Business, Huh!" The first of these meetings convened at Shearson's offices at 14 Wall Street on November 8, 1968, and there *Essence* magazine was born.

Few women attended the meetings. There were very few in corporate America at the time. But among the forty or fifty African-Americans who attended and who put forth their ideas for new business ventures was twenty-two-year-old Jonathan Blount, a salesman for the New Jersey Bell Yellow Pages. Blount announced that he had an idea for a Black women's magazine. The idea, he says, had come from his godmother, Claire Tarry, to whom he had confided his frustration with the way he was being treated on the job. "Why don't you start a business," she suggested. "What about a Black women's magazine?" He told her it had been tried. "Yes, but these are different times," she told him. The idea became more and more attractive to Jonathan, and eventually, he says, it became his passion.

Russ Goings introduced Jonathan Blount to several others who were present at those first meetings, including Ed Lewis, twenty-eight, who was a star in the executive training program at First National City Bank and whom Russ had tried to recruit to work for Shearson; Clarence Smith, thirty-five, one of the top salesmen at Prudential Insurance; Cecil Hollingsworth, twenty-eight, who had started a small printing brokerage firm; and Phillip Janniere, an advertising salesman for the *New York Times*. Russ and Mattie Goings continued to encourage the men to meet and to put together a business plan. The meetings were moved to First

Harlem Securities, and subsequently to a single rented room in a townhouse at 102 E. 30th Street in New York City, the office where Cecil Hollingsworth ran his printing brokerage business. There the five young men huddled every evening after work, without fail, to flesh out this idea of a women's magazine. Like other African-American pioneers before them, they improvised around their lack of financial resources. They decided to call themselves The Hollingsworth Group, for example, because Cecil Hollingsworth had Hollingsworth Group stationery left over from a previous business venture.

"What the business plan had to sell," says Russ Goings, "was five Black guys who had never published anything, with the hubris to go after the Black female market, and with no women involved." Fortunately, women did become involved. Cecil's wife, Pat Hollingsworth, became involved, conducting focus groups to cull ideas from young Black women about what they would want in a magazine. "One of the things we had to do," explains Cecil, "was qualify the idea and see if indeed there was a need for it. I had a neighbor who was a vice president of research at Young & Rubicam, and he helped us put together a questionnaire that Pat and a few other women used to conduct focus-group discussions on Saturdays."

Whether it was wisdom, good judgment, or stone-tapping blind-sight intuition that led them to seek Black women's input on the project early, the decision quickly proved an important one. Believe it or not, the working title for what would become *Essence* magazine was *Sapphire* (after the righteously indignant, neck-working, finger-shaking, hand-on-the-hip, and rolling-pin-upside-the-head wife of George "Kingfish" Stevens from the old "Amos 'n' Andy" television show of the early 1950s). "Who Is Sapphire?" the Hollingsworth Group's business plan asked rhetorically. Well, according to them . . .

Throughout most of her history in this country, she has had no realistic, complimentary images of herself either as a woman, or as a member of the community.

Nevertheless, in the past decade, she has undergone a transformation of self.

She has taken part in the struggle of all Black Americans for freedom, self-expression, self-determination, and full equality.

She has undergone a psychic and socio-economic revolution. Today's emerging Black woman has rejected the unfavorable and unflattering caricatures and stereotypes of her past and has sought and found her own true identities and images.

Today, she is Black and she is beautiful. And in her true self she has come to a new sense of self-worth, individuality, personal, and racial pride. She has in the truest sense come of age.

Sapphire is the magazine for the emerging Black woman.

We have named it *Sapphire* because, like the word "black," it has been transformed within the Black community from a term of disparagement to one of approbation. Within the Black community, it is the generic and idiomatic term for contemporary Black women.

The Hollingsworth Group had indeed targeted the *Essence* woman, but they had called her out of her name. Whatever transformation they thought *Sapphire* had undergone, she was apparently the same old Sapphire to Black women, who, in the focus group discussions, wisely counseled the brothers to "think about a new name."

With that advice, the partners—the four remaining partners—of the Hollingsworth Group decided to move forward with their business plan to try to raise $1.5 million to start this Black women's magazine. The fifth partner and first president of the group, Phillip Janniere, had decided to opt out of the venture in March of 1969 when developments required each to leave his job and commit full time to the project. Phillip didn't think they would be able to raise the money.

Ed Lewis recalls that there were nay sayers aplenty. "When I made the decision to leave First National City Bank [now named Citibank] to help start *Essence*, the head of the venture capital division at the bank, who had brought me into that division, said, 'Listen, this thing is going to fail. We're prepared to make you an officer.' But my position was that I was never going to be the chief executive of First National City Bank."

Adding to the risk, the partners initially decided not to accept salaries, which was a particular hardship for Smith and Hollingsworth, both of whom were married and had growing families. Clarence Smith says that his wife, Elaine, was at first very upset about the move and, quite frankly, frightened by it, but throughout the years she became his most ardent supporter. "I felt I needed to make a commitment to myself and to my wife that no matter what, I was personally going to make this business a success."

In April 1969, the partners became incorporated as the Hollingsworth Group, and the White magazine publishing industry actually rallied together to support the venture. The *New York Times* did a story on these four excited young men who were going to start a magazine targeted to Black women.

"There was a lot of euphoria in the country, a desire to do something," recalls Ed Lewis. "And as a result of us coming together to start this women's magazine, we were getting a lot of publicity, and a lot of people wanted to help."

"We had all these people helping us pro bono," says Clarence Smith. Magazine professionals were certainly offering tons of advice. But no financing was coming in. "The fact of the matter," says Clarence, was that "White folks were frightened to death of lending Black people money. They had very little background or experience in lending Black people money, especially to start up companies."

Finally, A. Michael Victory, executive vice president at Shearson, Hammill, introduced The Hollingsworth Group to three other principals from the Wall Street brokerage firm—Don Cecil, Walter Mintz, and Walter Maynard—who went into their own pockets, each lending the group $12,500.

OVERLEAF:
Black beauties: left to right, Joyce Walker, Charlene Dash, Naomi Sims, Barbara Cheeseboro, and Tamara Dobson appeared in an early advertisement for Essence.
May 1970

29

Come with ESSENCE into the full brilliance of your blackness.

In the pages of ESSENCE, each month I see myself. My heritage, my history, my folklore. My clothes, make-up, hair styles and accessories. My horoscope. And fiction. And poetry. Food for the soul. Soul food.

I have news of my people. And the changing scene. I find medical and psychological advice. And warnings of exploitation, over-pricing, gouging. Of uses and abuses.

I am alerted to the insurance racket, the burglar alarm racket, and to the social and economic dangers of drug addiction.

I meet the new black artists, composers, writers, photographers, actors, rhythm and blues groups, performers.

The Panther women. And Shirley Chisholm, Kathleen Cleaver, Aretha Franklin, Gwendolyn Brooks, Adrienne Kennedy, Fannie Lou Hamer, Mamie Clark.

I read about my children and their education. About new books. Movies. About travel. Vacations. About money. About jobs. About sex and love.

About anything, everything that "lifts the black woman high onto a pedestal and into the spotlight," in the words of **The Hollingsworth Group.**

Come into the brilliance of your own blackness.

She who is without ESSENCE is without soul.

While still trying to raise the money to start up the business, the group moved forward on faith, taking its first tentative steps from the mere concept of a magazine toward its realization. And for all the free advice they were given, they often found themselves feeling their way blindly. If they were going to start a magazine, they reasoned, they should have an editor-in-chief. Someone in the publishing industry suggested Bernadette Carey, who was a bona fide star at the *Washington Post*. She had worked for the *New York Times* women's news department, *Esquire*, and *Look*, and knew about general market magazines. Bernadette remembers the five of them putting in long hours, talking up the magazine, going to advertising meetings, trying to interest the advertising community, and, of course, trying to raise money.

"They began paying me as a kind of consultant while I was still in Washington," she recalls. "And I began collecting market research and putting together ideas for the magazine. We put together a dummy, and made up formats, story ideas, and issue plans, and sort of came up with the scope of the magazine."

Their excitement as they explored the possibilities of the magazine was part of the excitement of the times. Bernadette had definite ideas about the kind of voices for which she thought the magazine should provide a forum. "After the civil rights movement in the 1960s, there was a great explosion of young Black talent," she says. "Those were the days when Maya Angelou, Toni Morrison, and a lot of other writers were publishing their first books."

African-Americans were in fact making significant statements in a number of areas that Black women might find of interest in a magazine, among them, of course, fashion. As Bernadette notes, "Black women have always been interested in fashion and have helped set styles. And they were just beginning to break into modeling in the collections. There was also a group of young Black designers whom I'd met at the *New York Times*. There was just this enormous wealth of talent to be tapped."

Ed Lewis concurs. "We never thought it would be a 'fashion' magazine exclusively. We felt that we had to deal with some other issues above and beyond fashion because of what it meant to be a Black woman in this society. We had to be more a lifestyle magazine, a women's service magazine. Certainly fashion and beauty were part of it, but it is the totality that the magazine, in order to be relevant, had to address—what it is to be a woman with regard to work, with regard to where she lives, with regard to the importance of education, and what it is just to be a woman, a Black woman, in this society."

These were, and are still, real issues that need to be addressed. They are issues even for those who wish to provide a forum for them, as Bernadette and the partners discovered. "As one woman with four guys," she recalls, "it was for me not always so easy to explain some of the things that I felt were important in a women's magazine."

There were disagreements regarding the magazine's editorial direction and eventually Bernadette Carey left. She left, in fact, before the first issue was put together. In retrospect, twenty-five years later, she muses, "I really feel that in a certain way maybe they were right. The magazine has and does operate on a slightly different plane than if I had been the editor. After a while, it began to be less my baby and what it was in its own right. And as I watched that child grow up I still felt a great deal of pride and happiness and contentment at the fact that it existed. It's very satisfying to me, and it was a great joy to be editor-in-formation, which is really what I was."

Photographer-writer and soon-to-be director Gordon Parks was back and forth between New York and Hollywood, working on *The Learning Tree*, the film that marked his directorial debut, when he was contacted by The Hollingsworth Group and invited to join the staff of the magazine. Although his title was editorial director, he functioned generally as the creative director in the art department, selecting pictures. Gordon had worked five years at *Vogue* as a fashion photographer and had done documentary work at *Life* magazine. In fact, Gordon Parks had been the first African-American photographer to shoot for *Vogue* and for *Life*, and was about to become the first African-American to produce and direct at a major Hollywood studio. Gordon was involved with the magazine for just about a year. "I felt that it would take about that long to help get them established, and I did whatever I could. In my third floor office there was a big light table where I inspected a lot of the film that was coming in, then passed it on to the art director."

Ruth N. Ross, a former assistant editor at *Newsweek*, was brought in as the editor-in-chief of the magazine. She was young, smart, sophisticated, and very much a race woman. In a *New York Times* interview that ran February 11, 1970, she mused that no longer would she hear the all-too-familiar refrain, "But, Ruth, we already have one Black story in the back of the book." Unfortunately, Ruth was "too Black for prime time," and was let go after just one issue. Not, however, before she left her lasting mark on the magazine.

Over the years, no fewer than a dozen people and at least one research firm have claimed responsibility for naming *Essence*. But according to Ed Lewis, "The person who is responsible for naming the magazine "Essence" is Ruth Ross. We sat around at 102 East 30th Street trying to find a name because in focus-group discussions, Black women had said to us that the working title, *Sapphire*, 'cuts too deep.' We engaged a search firm, and we looked at hundreds of names, but it was Ruth Ross who said 'Essence.' I can tell you exactly who was at the meeting: It was Ruth, Clarence, Cecil, Jonathan, and me. There was a moment of silence. Then we said, 'Yes, yes! That's it!' We all just knew *Essence* was right."

Finally, the magazine had a name. What it didn't have was money. The money that had been loaned the Hollingsworth Group by the three gentlemen at Shearson had all too soon been eaten up by expenses, and the partners had, once again, found themselves at the end of their resources. Then, Freedom National Bank—a Harlem savings and loan which baseball legend Jackie Robinson helped establish—stepped in to save the day. "If it had not been for Freedom loaning us $30,000 to keep body and soul together in late 1969," says Ed Lewis, "we would not be talking about the 25th anniversary of *Essence* magazine today."

Reinvigorated, the group was out there with its business plan, trying to raise the $1.5 million. They made many presentations on Wall Street and secured several small loans from First National City Bank using the $1.5 million they hoped to raise as collateral. The problem was that by the time they sat down with Chase Manhattan Bank, First National City Bank, Morgan Guaranty, and several minority enterprise and small business investment companies (MESBICs) to close their first deal for $130,000 in March of 1970, First National City Bank had already loaned them roughly $167,000, and most of the money they collected at that first closing had to go to pay part of the First National City Bank obligation.

But somehow they managed to keep the business together, and *Essence* magazine made its debut in May 1970. The premier issue appeared on newsstands in 145 cities across the country with an initial press run of 175,000 copies, and Black Americans—in fact, all Americans who saw it—were stunned. Black women were jubilant. It was beautiful, serious, and a literary treat. *Essence* made its debut with such well-known writers as novelist Louise Meriwether, who contributed a piece on Black men and White women, and writer-actress Alice Childress on the meaning of Mother's Day for Black mothers whose children were being murdered by guns and drugs, and, ultimately, a corrupt system that willingly sacrifices them. Dr. Alvin Poussaint, professor of psychiatry at Harvard, discussed the psychological effects of racism and sexism on Black women. Leslie Alexander Lacy, a Black studies professor at Howard, contributed an analysis of what Black women say they want in Black men.

One of the cover headlines on that first issue, "Revolt: From Rosa To Kathleen," prefigured an article inside entitled "Five Shades of Militancy" by Gilbert Moore with photographs by Gordon Parks and Gordon Parks, Jr. The article featured such women in the struggle as Rosa Parks, Shirley Chisholm, and Kathleen Cleaver. This same article included Gordon Parks's now-famous photograph of a sea of women in white from the Nation of Islam.

Fashion pages in the magazine featured sisters in colorful geles and bright maxis and summer shorts, while other models in flesh-colored bodysuits posed with a muscular, ebony-black man with a shaved head. A piece on hair-styling offered tips on creating and caring for "Dynamite Afros." A moving image of Nina Simone, photographed in the blue light of the concert stage, accompanied an article on her stormy career. There were short pieces on Duke Ellington, Pharoah Sanders and Leon Thomas, and Melvin Van Peebles. There were

Norma Jean Darden, Trevor Stevens, and Barbara Cheeseboro, the earliest Essence *models.*
May 1970
Photo, Richard Noble

news updates on women in Tanzania who had taken to the streets to protest the custom of polygamy, on the Black Panthers, and on Angela Davis. Even the ads in the magazine featured Black models chosen from the rainbow of Black skin tones.

Essence had not only lived up to, but exceeded the expectations created by the media hype that had heralded its coming in *Time, Newsweek, Advertising Age,* and other publications. In a piece on the magazine's debut, the May 4, 1970, issue of *Time* described it as *Vogue*-cum-*Ramparts. Essence* couldn't even touch the radical *Ramparts,* but such hyperbole was commonplace in the context of the times, when the mere mention of racism in mixed company was sufficient to send defensive Whites to their windows and doors to shutter and bar them against militant Blacks who, they imagined, would come marching down on them in the next breath, armed with carbines and Molotov cocktails. According to *Time, Essence*'s "militancy carries over even into features on employment tips, travel, and a kind of Black Joyce Brothers psychiatric column." *Time*'s writers went on to predict that "After a while, *the young, urban, inquisitive and acquisitive Black woman* for whom the magazine is intended is going to get tired of being

Sisters in the Nation of Islam.
May 1970
Photo, Gordon Parks

reminded of *the long-standing, dehumanizing rape of the Black woman in America."*

She didn't have the chance. Even as the *Time* review was being written, Ruth Ross was probably cleaning out her desk and *Essence* editors were hurriedly revamping the second issue before sending it to press. *The Gallagher Report*, a Madison Avenue newsletter, warned that Black women's magazines have a "shaky future." The pressure was on. The next issue would be "more woman, less Black," nervous Whites (including investors) were assured.

The anxiety the *Essence* team had had over what the first issue should be was only heightened by the response of the national media, which apparently saw the magazine as a revolutionary organ seeking to incite Black women to Mau Mau acts of . . . who knows what. One of the problems was simply that there was no model for *Essence* before *Essence*. The partners of The Hollingsworth Group had risked everything, had given up their jobs and declined to take salaries to launch a Black women's magazine. And now there were just too many people fighting for control of the magazine's editorial voice.

"We were four young men, and we all considered ourselves publishers of the magazine," says Ed Lewis. "And that was very disorienting to the staff. Everybody was giving directives, the staff didn't know who to take direction from, and with all the different personalities that just created chaos."

Chaos—but a wonderful sort of chaos—is what Ida Lewis remembers finding when she was brought in as editor-in-chief following Ruth Ross's departure. "It was great fun, and sort of frightening because no one really knew what they were doing. You had four young men who had a vision, and we were all learning as we went. On the job learning. There was a lot of confusion, but also a lot of hope and excitement for the newness and freshness of the idea."

Ida had been living in France for five years, working first as a reporter for *Life* magazine and later as a freelance writer. She had also worked for the *Washington Post* and the BBC, had traveled to Africa, and had done stories as a freelancer for various publications in Europe, the Middle East, and Asia—one of very few women of any race writing and reporting on an international level. She was back in the states in 1968, covering the presidential election, when she got a call from Jonathan Blount. She was soon paid a visit by Jonathan, Cecil, Ed, and Clarence, who told her about the magazine and hired her almost on the spot. She repaid them the very next day with a visit to the *Essence* offices and ended up staying a year. When she arrived the first issue of *Essence* had already gone to press. When the second issue of the magazine came out in June of 1970, Ida Lewis's named appeared on the masthead as editor-in-chief.

"We worked constantly," she says of the staff that first year. She also notes that, in addition to the criticism coming from conservative White media, concern from investors, and the scrambling of an organization new to publishing trying to find its footing, there was yet another source of pressure. "This was a time when everyone had an ideology, and there were forces from the outside demanding that we focus the magazine in a certain direction. I mean politics surrounded us in every direction because you had people on the outside who had their vision of what the Black woman should be. And it was the men who were the most vocal, as if it were up to them to mold this whole new effort. I'm not talking about Ed, Clarence, Jonathan, and Cecil. I'm talking about the brothers in the community.

"At one point there was a group led by Sonny Carson, who is a friend of mine, who tried to take over the magazine. They came in—invaded the offices—and confronted us. Like, 'What are you about and what are you going to do? What kind of publication are you going to present to the Black community?' Telling us what we couldn't do and what we'd better do. So those kinds of forces were alive and well in the community. And I just wanted to do my job."

It was in the fall of that first year—1970—that I heard from my childhood friend Peggy Ruffin's brother, Steve Ruffin, and his partner, a photographer named Sonny Fraisier (now A. Raheem Sami), that *Essence* was looking for a beauty editor. I remember walking into the low-ceilinged basement offices on East 30th Street and into Ida Lewis's area—she didn't have an office and only an opaque screen separated Ida from her editorial staff. She hired me as a freelancer to begin to develop beauty stories for the magazine.

A few months later, in the early part of 1971, and unbeknownst to any of us on staff, "We came very close to closing *Essence*," says Ed Lewis, "because we didn't have any money to print the next issue. The wolf was at the door. I didn't know what

Five months after its debut issue, Essence *took the unusual step of showing in a national magazine a Black woman photographed in the nude.*
October 1970

to do and Michael Victory suggested that I talk to Louis Allen at Chase Manhattan. This was the guy who didn't even bring a check to the first closing. I called his secretary—a Black woman—who told me he was out of town, but was flying in from California, coming into Newark. I took the bus out to the airport and met him as he was coming down the ramp. He was shocked to see me, but I had his ear so I explained what the situation was—that we needed $50,000 or we were going to have to close the doors. He said, 'I'll swing with you one more time.' Years later, he said to me, 'That's when I knew you were serious about this business.'"

Later that year, *Playboy* magazine made a business decision to invest a quarter of a million dollars in *Essence*. Ed notes that other institutions had made small investments "designed to provide as little capital as possible and still get us to go away. But *Playboy* made a real investment." Sadly, *Essence* caught a lot of flack because of it, but that investment encouraged others. John Hancock Mutual Life Insurance Company invested $265,000, and ultimately Chase Manhattan became the largest investor in the magazine with $400,000. At that point, 1974, *Essence* had raised roughly $2 million.

Shortly thereafter, when Cecil Hollingsworth and the remaining partners disagreed about basic business philosophy and he left the partnership, the company changed its corporate name, from The Hollingsworth Group to Essence Communications, Inc.

But in 1970 and 1971, financing for the revolution in consciousness which *Essence* was fomenting in its pages was sporadic at best and nearly always inadequate. But despite the company's meager financial resources, the magazine grew visually and editorially rich. It was the first time we were seeing Black women of all shades in all our magnificence, wielding attitude and style from Sugar Hill in Harlem to the Champs-Elysée in Paris, where *Essence* traveled to shoot Black fashion models with berry-red lips, long, chocolate limbs, and natural hair waving like a jazz saxophone's warm vibrato; Black women were wrapped against the fall chill in burgundy, cinnamon, and rust-colored Moroccan capes and knee-high brown suede boots, striding the boulevard, laughing at boundaries. Some of the best photographers of the day went into the tenements where Black people are under siege to document in black and white and shades of gray the pain of Black women dying of drugs, and the hope inspired by the landslide election victory of Newark's first Black mayor, Kenneth Gibson. *Essence* talked about our lives from our perspective. There were profiles of activists, like Angela Davis, Eleanor Holmes Norton, and Amiri Baraka (then Leroi Jones); of artists like Barbara Chase-Riboud and Al Hollingsworth; of actors and singers Calvin Lockhart, Melba Moore, and Mahalia Jackson. *Essence* brought us conversations with Diana Sands, James Baldwin, Gwendolyn Brooks, and Soledad Brother George Jackson's letters from prison. There were essays written by Jesse Jackson, John Oliver Killens, and Nikki Giovanni. Historian John Henrik Clarke discussed the Black woman as a seminal figure in history. Pictorials of bejeweled Masai painted our pages in the ebony and red of the east African savannah. There were features on Black women in business and articles on breast feeding, diet, exercise, and travel.

Even the advertising pages spoke of Black pride, and one advertiser in particular, of a commitment to supporting Black business. "George Johnson, of Johnson Products, was our first big advertiser," notes Ed, "and was truly committed to assisting Black entrepreneurs in general, and us in particular. George made sure that Ultra Sheen and other Johnson Products would be in the magazine. He put his money where his mouth was."

In that first year, the foundation of the magazine was built, but not without temper tantrums, mass firings, walkouts, and division among the team. "Among the problems was the perception of the role played by Robert A. Gutwillig," says Clarence Smith. He was the person assigned by *Playboy* to the board to oversee *Playboy*'s investment in *Essence* which, at that time was a quarter of a million dollars, and was the biggest investment anyone had in the deal. Some members of the *Essence* partnership believed that Gutwillig was attempting to get control of the *Essence* board for *Playboy*." In that regard, his actions were construed as causing dissension and disparate views. And even though Gutwillig never did get control of the board, it was rumored by certain disgruntled factions that *Essence* was controlled by *Playboy*, which was not true, but which nevertheless caused a great deal of controversy for the company.

Ida Lewis remembers the internal politics, the struggles for control and power, and the constant jockeying for position, from the board and the partners down to the staff, none of which made putting out a magazine any easier. "All I wanted was to do my job. Bob Gutwillig, who represented *Playboy*'s interests on the board, would take me to lunch and talk about all of them, saying, 'Ida, if you want it, we can fix it so you can become a stockholder and you can have the magazine.' But, I mean it was just inconceivable to me that I would betray the men who had hired me, and that I would play along with the White side of it. I just couldn't do it."

The feuds and divisions and infighting that plague many fledgling businesses exacted their toll on *Essence*. By the end of that first year of *Essence* Ida Lewis was gone, Jonathan Blount was gone, a whole staff was gone. But despite all of that, the foundation was laid, and Black women accepted and supported the magazine. The magazine itself was beautiful, but it was still too narrowly focused and the audience was small, much smaller than what the partners had envisioned for it.

Beginning with the July 1971 issue, Marcia Ann Gillespie, who had been the managing editor under Ida Lewis, took over the magazine. Marcia had come to the magazine from Time-Life Books where she was a researcher. By 1970, after four years at Time, Inc., she was beginning to feel stymied.

"I was still at Time, Inc., when *Essence* was launched," she says. "Time-Life had a party to announce the launching of the magazine because Time had been part of that group of established publishers who were lending some sort of support to *Essence*. Ruth Ross, who was the editor-in-chief at that point, was there. Ed [Lewis] and Larry [Clarence Smith] were there. I had actually met Larry a year or so before when the magazine was called *Sapphire* and they were going around talking to women in the publishing business. So I crashed the party, and there were all these gorgeous Black people coming from far and near. I remember thinking, 'Wow, isn't this something?' Gordon Parks was there, and I knew Gordon because he was a photographer at *Life*. I said, 'Gordon, do you think maybe I could get a job over at *Essence*?' So Gordon was the one who facilitated the introduction."

Marcia, like many other women who have come to the magazine from other publications, took a cut in salary to work for *Essence*. Ida Lewis hired her, but

it was really Barbara Kerr who Marcia says made possible her incredible transition from researcher to managing editor. Barbara, who was a retired editor from *Mademoiselle*, had been brought to *Essence* because she had a lot of knowledge about magazines. "It was a humongous leap," Marcia says of the distance she traveled between researcher and managing editor, "but Barbara was an incredible teacher."

Marcia was an incredibly aggressive student as well. Even before Ida

BOTH PAGES AND OVERLEAF:
Essence *in Paris: the first fashion shoot abroad.*
October 1970
Photo, Helmut Newton

Lewis left the magazine, rumors began to circulate that Marcia was out to take over the publication from Ida. "I was not happy with the publication," she admits. "And I was young and I was very brash and thought I knew best. But it didn't hit me that I really wanted to be the editor-in-chief, I mean really, really wanted it, until after Ida was gone and the guys started interviewing other people. And they really had some reservations. They thought I was too young, they thought I was too brash. I had to state my case. Finally, the decision was made that I would be given a chance. So I was named editor. If you look at that first issue I did, you'll see that the masthead does not say editor-in-chief. I was named editor, with the *in-chief* to come if I proved I could do the job."

Marcia began to build a new team. She promoted me to fashion and beauty editor, and it was at that point that I joined the team full time.

Marcia brought to the task of refocusing the magazine's editorial direction a young, hip sensibility. Amazingly, she was only twenty-six years old when she became the editor-in-chief of *Essence*. But as Marcia recalls, "We were all so young, and it was like we knew we were inventing a new language."

She also brought to the job an insatiable curiosity which drove her to travel the country and meet people as few other Black women had at that time. She went south to Sunflower County, Mississippi, to interview Fannie Lou Hamer, to Chicago to interview Jesse Jackson. She traveled to big cities and small hamlets, speaking on college campuses and to Black women's organizations. Marcia talked to our readers, and the information she brought back about Black women from across the country gave the editors the basis for many groundbreaking articles. Marcia made *Essence* more relevant to everyday Black women. She made it a real service publication.

"It was energizing," she says. "I never came back from a trip where I didn't learn something I didn't know before. The thing, I think, that used to knock me over was to see how the work we were doing was making a difference in people's lives. The feedback and response I would get from the women, who really felt ownership of the magazine, was such confirmation."

"Marcia was very contemporaneous of her time," observes Clarence Smith. "But she also brought a historical perspective to the magazine. She was immensely bright, a history major at Lake Forest, and she was a young Black woman going through the whole civil rights experience at the time it was happening. So, two social forces came together and converged in Marcia, as they did in the nation at that time, and those two social forces were the apex of the Black struggle as it turned from Martin Luther King to Black power, and the fledgling women's movement which was getting started in the early 70s with the coming of *Ms.* magazine and Gloria Steinem and that whole group. Those two social forces

The more beaded necklaces, belts, rings, and armbands, the more festive the occasion in traditional Masai culture.
July 1970
Photo, Pete Turner

converged and were moving the nation in a different direction, and Marcia was right in the center of it. She was almost the perfect person to create the magazine that would be the spokesperson for Black women. And for nearly a decade that's what she did."

"I thought it was extraordinarily important that we always have a historical component," Marcia says of the magazine's editorial focus, "that we make sure we give that kind of grounding, because one could not assume that all of us knew our own history, which has been so denied us. I wasn't interested in what other women's magazines did, because women's magazines have been developed for a whole other kind of woman; one who had not come up through slavery, one who had not had to work, always work. One who had not been independent as Black women have been independent and on their own."

"I think Marcia really gave us the editorial credibility," says Ed Lewis. "Through her column, 'Getting Down,' she reached into the very soul of what it is to be a Black woman who is intelligent in this society. It was her personal odyssey, but it was also universal, and that was disseminated throughout the magazine."

When Marcia joined the magazine she felt it was still in search of itself. And she had very definite ideas about what *Essence* should be. "First and foremost, I thought it had to celebrate Black womanhood. I wanted to appeal to all the aspects of Black womanhood as I perceived it—you know, mind, body, and spirit. I wanted it to be multi-generational in its appeal. I wanted to have really good writing, because I believe we're incredibly smart people, and I wanted to include a range of subjects that we Black women had to think about and do something about. And I wanted the magazine to be more intimate. I wanted it to speak to how Black women really feel inside ourselves. I wanted the reader to talk to us, to feel like she was in conversation with us. I wanted her to feel ownership of the magazine, that it was hers."

Marcia accomplished all of those things. The writing remained strong, and the magazine became rich and unique. Her greatest legacy is that she molded the magazine to reflect the interests of a broad cross section of Black women.

Marcia's energy was part and parcel of the tremendous energy that came from everyone at *Essence* and permeated the offices every day, and would often keep us up half the night as Marcia herself reminded me. "Susan, I can remember you and me sitting up late at night or talking on the phone about everything—about mothers, about loves. And all of that was part of our personal growing up, but it usually translated into something for the magazine in some way.

"Audreen Ballard [editor, September 1975 to 1978] and I used to sit at the close of the day, in my office, looking out over the river, and just review, talk, and dream. But Audreen would also tell me what I didn't want to hear, which really pushed me, and sometimes I wanted to say 'Ee-nough!'

"Larry and I used to have classic fights. A lot of them were really the kind of church-state thing between advertising and editorial. But they were extraordinarily important because they helped me get clear about what the business was, where I should draw the line and what we could afford to compromise. Sometimes he was way off the wall, but then other times he was right. Because Larry nagged me all the time about our need to get food advertising, I added more food pages and created the Contemporary Living section. He pushed me to do something that I wouldn't have done—making a mini section in the back of the book which has proved to be a wonderful thing."

Marcia credits Ed Lewis with many things, not the least of which was letting her do the job. But the simple fact was that Ed learned a valuable lesson that first year when there were, as he says, "too many publishers."

"Leaving you alone to do what you wanted to do with the magazine," says Marcia, "and knowing, believing that you rose and fell on what you did; that was extraordinarily important."

Jim Forsythe, who joined *Essence* as circulation manager and today is senior vice president, director of circulation, is another one who Marcia says she used to fight with. "Jim and I would fight because I was more impatient than he was about expanding circulation. But Jim was not looking for just any number, but the right numbers. I remember this gorgeous cover we had put together with a beautiful chocolate woman in white fur with a blue background. Jim said, 'Marcia, don't run the cover.' I said, 'Are you crazy?' And he said, 'Blue and white covers don't sell.' Well, we ran it and it didn't sell. Later, he showed me the sales figure on blue and white covers going back over the years. A lot of what Jim taught me about circulation is still a part of my bible today. Jim knows the business. He knew how to grow the magazine, which is something I really wanted to see happen. I wanted *Essence* to grow."

Another great contributor in the early days of *Essence* was the late Sheila Younge, whom we called Miss Precise. Sheila was executive editor (July 1972 to October 1977) and a grammarian, whose oft-repeated advice to us was, "First you have to know the rules, then you can decide if you want to break them."

If *Essence* is anything, it is truly a tribute to Black creativity across a range of fields. It is a tribute to the writers, models, photographers, makeup artists, stylists, editors, to so many people whose names may not have appeared on the pages, but who contributed to the magazine, and who never would have been given a chance to create if not for *Essence*.

In early 1980, Marcia Gillespie moved on to other horizons. Today she is the editor-in-chief of *Ms.* magazine. "A lot of the things that we did at *Essence*, which I think are important, weren't things that I wanted to do anymore," she admits. "And I was tired. You know there are no sabbaticals in the business. But I'm always just incredibly grateful to have had that experience. It shaped and transformed me. And I think we have helped Black women, not just to see their beauty, but actualize it."

Daryl Royster Alexander followed Marcia Gillespie as editor-in-chief. Daryl had joined *Essence* in the early years, had left for a short period when her husband accepted a job in Atlanta, and then returned to work with Marcia again as the editor. She was smart, a good writer, and a hard worker. But I know now that being a wife and mother and trying to step into Marcia's shoes must have been totally overwhelming at times. It's a seven-day-a-week, 18-hour-a-day, 24-hour-on-call job. After a year, Daryl moved on to the *New York Times*. But she provided a bridge between Marcia's stewardship and mine.

Once it was known that Daryl would be moving on, Ed Lewis came to me and said that he was considering me for the position. I assumed he was kidding, of course. I was a high school graduate, in awe of the women I worked with who had advanced degrees from some of the finest colleges and universities. I had been fashion and beauty editor for ten years, not executive editor, not managing editor, not even an associate editor. And the thought of ever becoming editor-in-chief was so far beyond anything I had ever imagined for myself that it seemed a ridiculous idea, which is precisely what most everyone inside and outside of *Essence* felt when later it was announced.

Ed recalls, "I had asked Marcia when she was first thinking about leaving, 'What about Susan?'" Marcia's response was that I was not quite ready yet, but might be in a couple of years.

I soon realized that Ed was serious, and so, after giving it some serious thought myself, I said, "I'm ready. When do I start?" But it wasn't going to be that simple. Clarence had some reservations, and Ed had only his instincts to recommend me.

"We had reached out to a number of top journalists," says Clarence, "and when Ed mentioned Susan, I said, 'How do we know she can do the job?' And Ed just had a feeling about it. So I suggested we give you a test." They asked me to put together a document describing my vision for the magazine, and gave me a month in which to do it. In a single long weekend, over the New Year's holiday, I put together three documents: my editorial philosophy; the editorial direction, which included issue plans and ideas for articles, and a description of the kind of graphics that would define the look of the magazine; and an analysis of the synergy between advertising and editorial. Recently, Clarence told me that when he read what I had put together, he had told Ed, "Let's give her the job."

In 1981 when I became editor-in-chief of the magazine there were two factors that helped me to build successfully upon Marcia's legacy. One, I was a single mother wrestling with what seemed like so many competing pressures: trying to raise my daughter, stave off bill collectors, meet my many work-related deadlines, handle a difficult love relationship. I was trying to maintain my balance, to not lose my footing. My life, like the lives of many Black women, was a struggle. I felt very much in touch with *Essence* readers' needs and interests—so many of which mirrored my own. And two, I knew enough to seek out, hire, or promote over the years the smartest people I could find: Expert editors Audrey Edwards,

Essence publisher Ed Lewis, president Clarence O. Smith, and the staff rejoice in the holiday spirit. Left to right, row 1: Sheila F. Younge, executive editor; Alexander B. Mapp, art director; Marcia A. Gillespie, editor-in-chief; Susan L. Taylor, fashion and beauty editor; row 2: Maria Davis, receptionist; Clarence O. Smith, president; Ed Lewis, publisher; Cecil Hollingsworth, vice-president; row 3: Denise McDonald, fashion and beauty asst.; Sharyn J. Skeeter, fiction and poetry editor; Frances E. Ruffin, associate editor; Len Taylor, promotion director; Joel Reiss, production manager; Jim Forsythe, market analyst; Ann Lacey, administrative asst.; Tom Rivers, advertising; row 4: Emma McKnight Edwards, copy editor; Toni Greene, administrative asst.; Craig DaCosta, advertising; Yayoi Tsuchitani, asst. art director; Raymond Joseph, asst. treasurer; Sandra Nelson, administrative asst.; row 5: Ronald Prester, accounting; Kamu Mistry, accounting; Joseph R. Calim, advertising; Kathy Shaw, advertising; top: Reginald Ashe, accounting. December 1972 Photo, Si Chi Ko

Charlotte Wiggers, Cheryll Greene, Stephanie Stokes Oliver, Linda Villarosa, Valerie Wilson Wesley, Pamela Johnson, Diane Weathers, and Gordon Chambers; talented art directors and designers Fo Wilson, Gregory Gray, Marlowe Goodson, Janice Wheeler, and LaVon Leak-Wilks; fashion and beauty editors Sandra Martin, Mikki Taylor, Ionia Dunn Lee, and Harriette Cole. Master public relations professional Terrie Williams and promotions genius Karen Thomas became tremendous supports when they joined the *Essence* family.

Even so, because the dreams of Ed Lewis and Clarence Smith are constantly expanding beyond the fields of expertise of a relatively small staff, each of us has had to wear a number of hats. Each of us has had to walk a mile in shoes which were at first too big. Each of us has been given responsibilities that forced us to grow.

Working on the magazine pushed, stretched, and challenged me. I always felt that I had to do more and be more just to keep up with the awesome women with whom I've worked over the years. Working with intelligent, dynamic, and confident women made me want to tap into those same qualities in myself. If not for the challenges presented by my expanding role within Essence Communications, Inc., our parent company, I might never have gone back to school to get a college education. The responsibility of representing the magazine pushed me, usually with great reluctance, into areas in which I initially felt insecure and inadequate. One of the great fears I had after being named editor-in-chief was having to write a monthly editorial. I wanted to eliminate it from the magazine, but Ed Lewis said that if I wanted to be editor-in-chief I had to write a monthly column. So I began writing about what I care about most, the transforming power of the divine within us. Never did I dream that "In the Spirit" would be embraced to the degree that it has been by our readers, or that it would become a popular book for *Essence*. Like Marcia, I made it part of my mandate to travel the country, visiting college campuses, women's groups, and community-based organizations, and as a result I found myself doing public speaking, something I was initially terrified of doing.

I have seen "Essence" the television program, a show I hosted and helped produce, become the first African-American–owned nationally syndicated magazine show. Over the years we have sent expeditions of editors, writers, and photographers to many African nations, to Europe, Asia, and throughout the Caribbean to tell the stories of our people. I've had the opportunity to travel throughout much of the world and have had the joy of being received in so many arenas—at inner city street festivals, at the White House, and by heads of state throughout the world. So often I have felt overwhelmed by the responsibilities and the challenges of being a spokesperson for *Essence*, but always thankful, and always excited about the possibilities that our company, which is committed to moving Black people forward, holds for people of African ancestry throughout the world.

Throughout the years there have been takeover attempts, misappropriation of corporate opportunities, fights between the partners, and a whole host of things that could have shattered the dream, but the core held together. Throughout all of it, Ed Lewis and Clarence Smith have hung in there together, bound by the larger purpose of the mission, and *Essence* has survived and the company has grown.

Today, Essence is a communications and merchandising company with interests in television and print media. *Essence* magazine has become a source of information and pride to Black women throughout the world, with more than five million readers in the U.S. and a growing readership in Canada, the Caribbean, Great Britain, and English-speaking African countries. And it has unearthed for advertisers the demographic that African-Americans have known was there all along. The nationally televised "Essence Awards" have aired annually on network television since 1992. The company owns and publishes *Income Opportunities* magazine, an acquisition which represents the first time a Black-owned publishing company has bought a general market magazine from a White-owned concern. Essence also is a major shareholder in Amistad, a publishing company. Essence has established an identity that Black women, and men, have embraced as a sign of quality. Essence Communications has a mail-order catalogue business, and today the Essence name is on patterns, hosiery, and eyewear. Essence Art produces and sells art prints. As we move toward the second millennium, "Our goal," as Ed Lewis often says, "is to become a corporate empire."

As a girl growing up in Harlem, I had dreams, but never of anything quite this magnificent—working to help enrich the lives of Black women. This mission has made every waking, working, purpose-filled moment a joy, and I am grateful. I am grateful to Ed Lewis for believing in me when I didn't believe in myself. I am grateful to God for the opportunity to do this great work. I am grateful.

The images in this book are a celebration of the beauty, the attitude, and style of Black women as *Essence* has documented us over the past twenty-five years. The idea for this book was originally suggested some years ago by Gregory Gray, who was the art director at the time. It has come to fruition through the efforts of Joan Sandler, an old and dear friend of *Essence* who pursued the idea and brought the deal to the table; the vision and tenacity of editor Patricia Hinds; and the hard work of so many others, including Stephanie Stokes Oliver, Marlene Connor, and my loving husband, Khephra Burns.

How do we assess an epoch, define a generation, or sum up twenty-five years in the cosmic span of eternal history? By what standard do we record the measure of our progress or chart the moral and philosophical distance traveled to seize the prize? For the past twenty-five years the keeper of the record and the flame, the griot charged with telling and continuing the story, has been Essence magazine, the publication launched in 1970 to reflect the very heart, soul, spirit, and beauty of Black womanhood. During the last two and one-half decades Essence has celebrated personal achievements, chronicled social movements, documented struggles, showcased beauty, defined and set trends, and tracked the incredible journey of a resilient and splendid race of women over the vagaries of time and circumstance.

In this celebration we reflect on the history of Black women during the past twenty-five years in the areas of personal achievement, personal style, beauty, interpersonal relationships, and spiritual development. Highlighted are the accomplishments of some individual Black women whose daring, vision, and talents have contributed to the collective good of us all. Through such women we can take the measure of our success and celebrate the victory.

Our Style

Style. The way we do the things we do. Be it swing or be-bop, jazz or hip-hop; the strut of Black models on the runway or the beat of Black girls jumping double Dutch, American style has invariably been shaped by "a Black thing." In fashion, in music, in sports, and the arts, it is typically a Black style that breaks the rules, reinvents the game, and sets new standards. We are, after all, the people who make a way out of no way and believe in the evidence of things not seen.

We came into the last third of the twentieth century turning American style on its ear. We sported huge Afros and slick curly perms, wore rings in our noses and beads in our hair. We've teetered on platform shoes and preened in silk dashikis. We have suited up for the corporation and been pressed in the neighborhood. We are Buppies and fly girls, sisters in the Nation, and comrades in the struggle. We can be prim and proper one minute, give attitude and talk trash the next. Shoop. Shoop. Our distinctive style has always given Black expression—indeed, Black life—its singular vitality.

This vitality would emerge full force in an era marked as much by changing styles as by changing politics. And fashion became a barometer of both style and changing times. Not surprisingly, fashion has been an important part of *Essence* since it debuted in May 1970. Our beauty and style had never been showcased in its full panoramic glory, nor had our Black models or Black fashion designers been given an adequate stage to work their magic. *Essence* has provided the forum for both during the past twenty-five years.

Living proof of the "Black is Beautiful" credo that greeted the seventies was the bevy of Black models who suddenly graced the pages of American magazines. Naomi Sims was the first Black model to appear on the covers of *Ladies Home Journal* in 1968 and *Life* in 1969. And her African-American aristocratic beauty would pave the way for other brown-skinned beauties such as Beverly Johnson, who was the first Black model on the cover of *Vogue* magazine in 1974, Barbara Smith and Billie Blair in the seventies, and Mounia, Naomi Campbell, and Roshumba in the eighties and nineties.

Black turned out to be not just beautiful but quite stunning in high fashion as well. There was something about the play of vibrant skin color against the colors of cloth. There was something about the way Black women moved—down the street or down the runway—that conveyed attitude and that certain indefinable quality known as style. It was this certain something that caught Givenchy's eye and led him to choose mostly Black models to present his collections.

Amazing Grace Jones, model, actress, personality-plus, has always been over the cutting edge of the beauty, fashion, and music industries.
June 1985

Black designers would also come into vogue during the last quarter of the century. Though it was Black men such as Stephen Burrows, Willi Smith, Scott Barrie, and Patrick Kelly who made their marks on the fashion scene during the seventies and eighties, as well as Tracy Reese, the young Black woman who worked for Magaschoni and has become a top designer in her own right in the nineties, it was always the Black female form that gave designer clothes style and power.

Willi Smith's favorite model was his own sister, Toukie Smith, who wore his all-American classic khaki jackets and pants, skirts, and jumpers with an elegant abandon that marked urban style. Toukie would go on to have a career as a model and actress, and then later establish the Smith Family Foundation in honor of her brother, who died from AIDS. Her tireless fundraising efforts together with her other business ventures epitomized the new Black models of the last twenty-five years: not just pretty faces, but women who took their sense of personal style and taste into the entrepreneurial arena when their modeling tenure was over and launched new successful careers. A line of cosmetics and wigs bears Naomi Sims's name. Bethann Management Company, Inc., is the international modeling agency headed by Bethann Hardison, who has been pivotal in organizing Black models around such issues as equitable Black representation in fashion magazines and catalogues. Peggy Dillard opened a hair salon in Harlem in the eighties. Barbara Smith became a successful restaurateur. And Iman debuted with a line of cosmetics in the nineties with phenomenal success its very first month on the market, thus becoming one of the most successful cosmetic launches of all time.

What Black women have always proven is that style knows no limits of age or profession, rank or income. Style is Lena Horne at seventy-seven or Judith Jamison at fifty-one. It is Mae Jemison, the doctor of medicine who became an astronaut, or Johnnetta B. Cole, the doctor of anthropology who became a college president. It is the Delaney sisters, Sarah and A. Elizabeth, strong and feisty and independent at over one hundred years young. It is Florence Griffith Joyner flashing tie-dyed spandex and sequined nail tips as she sprints in first place across the finish line. It is Patti LaBelle hitting the high note.

In these closing days of the millennium Black American style would take on a distinctly African flavor. Kente and mud cloth have become the patterns of a new aesthetic in fashion. We now take African names later in life, or give them to our children immediately at birth. We celebrate Kwanzaa, jump the broom, and pour libations to the ancestors.

What has perhaps been most historic about these last twenty-five years is that we have come full circle as a people: found our roots, returned to the source, and emerged to embody the very essence of both Old and New World style.

Tony Award-winner Melba Moore encircles her face in color.
July 1970
Photo, Jon Naar

The jersey gown shown on the magazine's first anniversary issue cover was designed especially for Essence *by the late Scott Barrie.*
May 1971
Photo, Anthony Barboza

During the 1950s, Dorothea Towles made her mark in Paris as one of the first women of color to earn a living as a fashion model.
January 1987
Photo, Gregory Kent
Photo courtesy of the Barbara Lakesmith Collection at the Schomburg Center for Research in Black Culture, New York Public Library

In the 1950s, Helen Williams was the first brown-skinned model to achieve national prominence.
January 1987
Photo, courtesy of the Barbara Lakesmith Collection at the Schomburg Center for Research in Black Culture, New York Public Library. Photo, courtesy of Helen Williams

Vee-Form by Modess.... *because anatomically shaped*

Svelte and sophisticated, supermodel Naomi Sims was a pioneer of the fashion industry.
January 1987
Photo, Nesti

My personal style is my personal style. When they put you in that box and lower you six feet down, you go in alone. Nobody goes with you. If you don't recognize this while you're alive—recognize that it is your responsibility, yours and not others', to make you happy—you'll never make it. I've learned that if I try to please others and not me, I'll never find my own happiness.

—Diahann Carroll, "About Diahann Carroll" by Alan Ebert, July 1974

OVERLEAF:
The beauty of contrasting white.
July 1982
Photo, Hank Londoner

*Get back! Supermodel Tyra
Banks wearing a whispery
sheer silk cocoon in St.
Croix.
June 1992
Photo, Marc Baptiste*

*Bias-cut slip that works
under business wear by day
becomes a dress by night.
November 1980
Photo, Denis Piel*

*One of the first nose rings
ever featured in a magazine
as a fashion accessory, it
was dramatic and
revolutionary.
May 1970
Photo, Tomas*

OPPOSITE:

*Naomi Campbell and friend
cooling it in Cancun.
April 1991
Photo, Bolling Powell*

67

Jon Haggins designs for the
woman who is "self-assured
and wants to be noticed."
October 1988
Photo, Buckmaster

Designer Lester Hayatt's
fashions first appeared in
the late seventies.
October 1988
Photo, Buckmaster

We'll never forget him.
Patrick Kelly, Mississippi
homeboy, was the first
American asked to join
France's Chambre
Syndicale, the prestigious
French designers'
organization.
October 1988
Photo, Nesti

69

ABOVE:

The style was very seventies and very sexy.
July 1970
Photo, Mel Dixon

TOP RIGHT:

The investment pantsuit: oversized blazer and matching ankle-cropped topstitched trousers.
September 1982
Photo, Jacques Malignon

Elegant and sensual nightgowns were called honeymoon killers.
April 1973
Photo, Owen Brown

OPPOSITE ABOVE:

Model Wanakee in classic knit fashion. Works of art by Murat Brierre and Georges Liataud at Harlem's Studio Museum.
February 1983
Photo, Anthony Barboza

OPPOSITE BELOW:

Fall takes a fluid form with draped dress on Mounia. Herbert Gentry's In the Garden *is in the background.*
February 1983
Photo, Anthony Barboza

The magazine has always recognized the beauty of age and wisdom. Sarah and Elizabeth Delany, both 100 plus, are authors of the bestseller Having Our Say. *January 1994 Photo, Matthew Jordan Smith*

Novella Nelson, actress, models dramatic textiles designed by Mozelle Forte. February 1974 Photo, Ken Mori

OPPOSITE:

*From Stephen Burrows:
free-falling black matte
jersey glorified by Nefertiti-
type cuffs.
September 1970
Photo, Silano*

*Essence was the first to
present accessories shown in
unconventional ways on
Black bodies.
May 1970
Photo, Richard Noble*

*Stephen Burrows's neon
bright shades fall into place
on a slinky midi.
September 1970
Photo, Silano*

Essence *went to Senegal for its first African journey.*
July 1978
Photos, Anthony Barboza

BOTTOM RIGHT:
In Senegal Essence *captured the spirit of its women who take pride in their style, work, and traditions.*
July 1978
Photo, Seiji Kakizaki

A 1970s look: peacock feathers.
April 1974
Photo, Manny Gonzalez

Unforgettable Iman brought in the New Year with exquisite Afrocentric style.
January 1988
Photo, Buckmaster

NEAR LEFT:
Iman.
September 1985
Photo, Bob Kiss

FAR LEFT:
Iman, unearthing our natural beauty with fashion's newest twilight tones.
September 1981
Photo, Jacques Malignon

OPPOSITE:
Iman, who is from Mogadisho, Somalia, holds the motherland near—in Jamaica.
July 1980
Photo, Mel Dixon

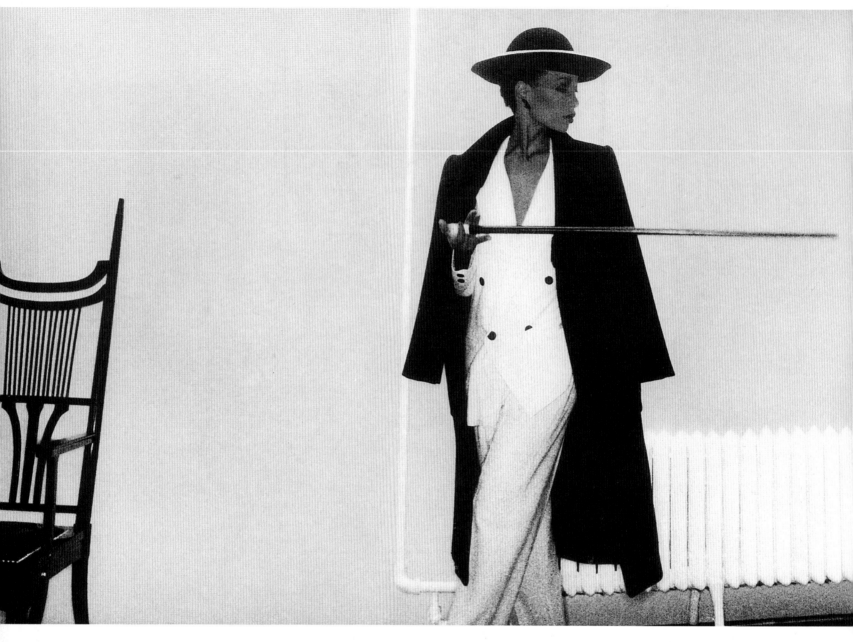

Black-and-white attitude
on supermodel Mounia.
October 1982
Photo, Robert Lambert

NEAR RIGHT:
Jon Haggins's draped-back
chemise on Mounia.
October 1982
Photo, Robert Lambert

FAR RIGHT:
Mounia in head-to-toe
elements of lush layers.
October 1982
Photo, Robert Lambert

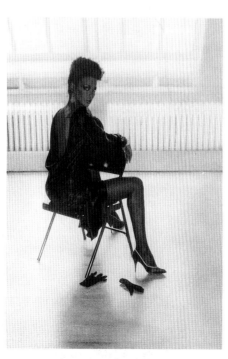

OPPOSITE ABOVE:
Mounia facing fall with
great style. Totem by Grace
Williams.
October 1982
Photo, Robert Lambert

OPPOSITE BELOW:
Majestic Mounia.
October 1982
Photo, Robert Lambert

I read about the death of Josephine Baker, like everyone else in Paris, with my morning coffee. I had met her only once, at one of her innumerable farewell performances that had been held regularly for the last twenty years. This performance at Paris's Olympia Theatre in 1968 featured, for the first part of the program, dancers Carmen Delavallade and Geoffrey Holder. I was backstage with them when I met her.

I thought, "Anybody's aunt from St. Louis. What is all the fuss about?" The bright but melancholy eyes, the extravagant eyelashes behind bifocals, the aging jowls, the slight dowager's hump, the small, rather dumpy figure looked ridiculous in the chorus-girl costume cut high into the hip. Yet in the midst of a rather grandmotherly conversation La Josephine, then 64, received her cue to go onstage. And before my unbelieving eyes, the superstar emerged from the frump and folds of age.

She appeared to shed pounds. The line of her back straightened, her upper thighs tensed and lengthened, her stomach flattened, her jowls disappeared. Her eyeglasses were hurriedly exchanged for a rhinestone microphone, her chin lifted, her head went back, and the Josephine of Parisian dreams suddenly appeared as if by magic onstage. A huge and collective sexual sigh seemed to rise from the audience upon her entrance, the smooth siren voice slid out over the audience. I turned to Geoffrey in amazement. He just shrugged his shoulders and said, "I told you she was something else."

—Barbara Chase Riboud, "Josephine Baker," February 1976

I hate the word. Star. Ugh! What broad in her right mind would rather be that than a woman? This crazy business often forces a gal to make that choice. But not me. Status never did do for me. It's not what you have materially or what titles are attached to your name that matters, but who you are as a person.

—Sarah Vaughan, "Still Sassy" by Alan Ebert, October 1974

Now I am not opposed to sophistication per se, but when you lose touch with your mama, when you take the word of an absolute, hostile stranger over and above the unarguable truth of your own miraculous, hard-won history, and when you don't remember to ask, again and again, "Compared to what?" I think you don't need to worry about enemies anymore. You'd better just worry about yourself.

—June Jordan, "Don't Talk About My Mama!" December 1987

Lashing out with bold gold accents.
July 1987
Photo, Reneé Cox

OPPOSITE:

Model Wanakee in timeless
nautical stripes.
October 1984
Photo, Bobby Holland

Mounia, one of Yves Saint
Laurent's favorite models.
January 1987

LEFT, AND OPPOSITE:
Haute couture: Fashion
in Paris.
October 1987
Photos, Reneé Cox

The ultimate in Sunday
hats makes high style.
May 1987
Photo, Nesti

An organza and taffeta
wedding dream from Vogue
Patterns.
February 1987
Photo, Isabel Snyder

FAR LEFT:
Designer Adrienne
McDonald's fitted jacket
with sheer palazzo pants.
February 1992
Photo, Tom Sullivan

NEAR LEFT:
For the bride, Kevan Hall's
beaded dance dress topped
with Hugo Redwood's
swing coat.
February 1992
Photo, Tom Sullivan

*The futuristic bride heeds
the call for shorter hemlines
in a strapless dress with
triple-tiered petal skirt.
February 1988
Photo, Reneé Cox*

RIGHT:
*The New Wave bride tosses
tradition to the wind in Jon
Haggins's bodysuit under a
bowed skirt.
February 1988
Photo, Reneé Cox*

ABOVE:

Haitian model Marguerite Erasme with holiday attitude.
December 1979
Photo, Gary Gross

LEFT:

Black velvet bustier dress lavished with gold lamé ruffles.
December 1987
Photo, Isabel Snyder

OPPOSITE:

Kwanzaa, the seven-day observance of principles relating to self, family, and community development, is a joyous time to celebrate in regal holiday style. Senufo statue from Ivory Coast.
December 1989
Photo, Reneé Cox

Our Achievements

No social phenomenon has more dramatically defined the last twenty-five years in American history than the two revolutionary movements for human rights that ascended back-to-back, overlapped, at times collided, but in the end empowered both a race and a gender. It was clearly the Black woman who stood most transformed by the dual social forces of civil rights and women's liberation that marked this era. She emerged at the dawn of the seventies tempered by the civil rights struggles of the fifties and sixties, primed to bear witness to the final days of the second millennium. She would usher in the turbulent womanist decade of the seventies, squarely face the roaring backlash decade of the eighties, and end the closing decade of the nineties with neither a bang nor a whimper, but simply an astonishing sense of her own power.

What has been most remarkable about the last quarter century is the extent to which Black women have so stunningly come into their own—as leaders, thinkers, artists, politicians, community activists, businesswomen, athletes, and arbiters of fashion and taste, style and beauty. In a single generation, women who once toiled in the fields would now change history by helping set a national agenda.

The decade of the seventies opened with the starting gun of the explosive civil rights sixties still hot and smoldering. A little pistol from Brooklyn named Shirley Chisholm became the first Black woman elected to Congress when she was voted into the U.S. House of Representatives in 1968. Her steely presence in the halls of power complemented that of another firebrand, Fannie Lou Hamer, the Mississippi sharecropper who became a legendary activist and would take her southern struggle for civil rights to the very steps of the Democratic party. When she arrived in Atlantic City during the summer of 1964, leading a posse of grassroots delegates to the Democratic National Convention, Hamer was hoisting the banner of the Mississippi Freedom Democratic Party—and daring to put the U.S. political process on notice: If the parties of Abraham Lincoln and Franklin D. Roosevelt could not find a way to accommodate the interests of its Blacks and its women, the constituency of outsiders would have no choice but to create its own third party. The challenge set the stage for the 1972 Democratic National Convention in Miami in which Shirley Chisholm's name was put into nomination for U.S. president on the first ballot, the first Black person to seek a major party nomination. America's two-party system has not been the same since.

Black women have clearly become an undeniable factor in the American political equation during the last twenty-five years, with ten Black women in the

Shirley Chisholm, the first Black U.S. Congresswoman, earned the reputation "unbought and unbossed," which also served as the title of her autobiography. May 1970
Photo, Gordon Parks

Fannie Lou Hamer, one of the great African-American freedom fighters, ran for the State Senate in Mississippi.
October 1971
Photo, Lou Draper

Barbara Jordan blazed through the governmental ranks in Texas to serve as a State Senator and Congresswoman.
September 1977
Photo, Fred J. Maroon

RIGHT:

Congresswoman Maxine Waters from California parlays her national platform into progress.
November 1990
Photo, Peter Darley Miller

U.S. Congress by 1995, including our first United States Senator, Carol Moseley-Braun from Illinois, and the indomitable California representative Maxine Waters, whose no-nonsense manner and uncompromising style have made her a formidable champion for her South Central Los Angeles constituency. There were also sixty-nine Black women mayors running American cities in 1993 (up from twenty-nine in 1984), among them Washington, D.C., Mayor Sharon Pratt Kelly, the first Black woman to preside over a major U.S. city and the nation's capitol. The Clinton administration brought firsts with a Black woman Surgeon General of the U.S. Public Health Service, the bold and spirited M. Joycelyn Elders, articulating a national health agenda; and a U.S. Secretary of Energy, Hazel O'Leary, setting the country's energy policy. And in the late 1970s there was Patricia Roberts Harris, the first Black woman appointed to a U.S. cabinet position when she was named secretary of Housing and Urban Development in 1977 by President Carter.

It was a Black woman, Barbara Jordan, the formidable congresswoman from Texas, who brought grace and stature to the historic and sticky business of conducting impeachment hearings on Richard Nixon in 1974. When she leaned into the microphone from her seat on the Judiciary Committee to explain the articles of impeachment, it was with such eloquence, passion, and precision that a nation was stunned into confronting the unthinkable: an American president was about to be brought down. And sounding the death knell was a lone Black woman who became our best metaphor for the changing of the guard.

Nearly twenty years later another Black woman, Maya Angelou, would stand before the American public to help usher in a new presidency and confirm just how much the guard had changed. The choice of a Black woman by President Bill Clinton to create and read an original work of poetry during his swearing-in ceremony in January 1993 was not just politically correct, but a fitting tribute to the rich contributions Black women have made in arts and letters. In 1950, Chicago writer Gwendolyn Brooks became the first African-American awarded the Pulitzer Prize for her poetry, and forty-three years later novelist Toni Morrison, who has given us such wonderful works as *The Bluest Eye, Sula, Song of Solomon, Tar Baby, Beloved,* and *Jazz,* was honored as the first African-American to receive the Nobel Prize for literature. That same year, 1993, Rita Dove, who won a Pulitzer prize for poetry in 1987, became the first Black American appointed Poet Laureate of the U.S.

In between those decades we witnessed novelist Alice Walker receive both an American Book Award and a Pulitzer Prize in 1983 for her extraordinary book *The Color Purple,* which was also made into an award-winning motion picture. Author Terry McMillan elevated the Black romance to blockbuster status with her

It's been an exciting time to be a Black woman writer. Trips to the bookstore became not exercises in frustration or forays into the wasteland, but a rich cornucopia of possibilities and promise. We had novels to peruse, autobiographies to provide life lessons, poetry to lift us, and spiritual guidebooks to clarify the journey we had chosen. We had our sisters' voices around us, speaking to and for and with us in ways we had never had before, and we rose to the challenge, buying books in unprecedented numbers, and adding a new category to the list of significant "market segments among the book-buying public": African-American women.

We nodded conspiratorially to each other as we read our hardbacks on rush hour subway trains. We bought multiple copies of our favorites so our gentleman friends could keep up. We sent copies in the mail to our faraway sisters so that we could compare notes and laugh about how much these books sounded just like we sounded, in all our loving confusion and persistent complexity and breathtaking determination.

We embraced this new Renaissance with a fervor that fed our sisterwriters in their work. They felt our energy and the fruits of their labors were our reward. A new day was clearly at hand and our only regret was that Zora Neale Hurston wasn't around to enjoy it.

But one of the good things about being a Black woman writer is that there isn't much time for regrets. We still have too much work to do; too many stories to tell; too many readers to provoke and delight and enlighten. I think Zora would be proud.

—Pearl Cleage, August 1994

My judgments are harsh because I had nothing to measure them against. It was a great shock to me when things began to die off because to me that was the way life was—people marching, picketing, carrying on and sitting in. And so to me an abnormal state is not doing that. Some people took that seriously. The young people especially. I was one of them. I was at an age when you just don't filter, when you accept things as gospel. And that was part of the disappointment. Adolescents think in a very humorless way. Either you come through or you don't.

—Michele Wallace, "Macho Myths and Michele Wallace"
by Marcia Ann Gillespie, August 1979

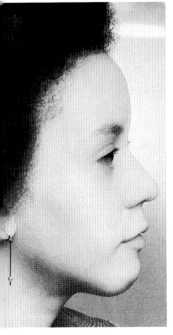

CLOCKWISE FROM FAR LEFT:

*Verta-Mae Grosvenor,
author and cultural
historian, on Amelia Island.
July 1982
Photo, Hank Londoner*

*Pearl Cleage's bold and
spirited writing has been
well received by* Essence
*readers.
February 1989
Photo, Nancy Nolan*

*Author Michele Wallace
tackled taboos with* Black
Macho & the Myth of the
Superwoman.
*August 1979
Photo, William Coupon*

*Nikki Giovanni, renowned
poet, was one of the first
voices to celebrate Black
beauty, spirit, power, and
history.
August 1970
Photo, John Vidol*

pot boiler novel *Waiting to Exhale*, which by summer 1994 had sold over 700,000 copies in hardback (remaining on the *New York Times* best-seller list thirty-eight weeks), and one million copies during the first month it was released in paperback in 1993. And then Walker and McMillan, together with Toni Morrison, made literary history when their respective books, *Possessing the Secret of Joy*, *Waiting to Exhale*, and *Jazz*, appeared simultaneously on the *New York Times* best-seller list in 1992, offering exquisite proof of just how popular and enduring the lives of Black women had become by the end of the century.

Terry McMillan's page-turning sister wit in Waiting to Exhale *and other novels made publishing history and set off an explosion in books by Black authors.*
October 1992
Photo, Monica Lee

Reporting with eloquence and passion the stories of those lives for more than twenty-five years has been journalist Charlayne Hunter-Gault, national correspondent of PBS's "The MacNeil/Lehrer NewsHour." Hunter-Gault, whose work has earned her two Emmy Awards and the George Foster Peabody Broadcast Award, was also the first Black woman to integrate the University of Georgia in 1961. And Isabel Wilkerson, Chicago bureau chief of the *New York Times*, became the first Black woman to win a Pulitzer Prize for journalism in 1994 for her feature writing. We have also been blessed during this last quarter century to have had the rich voice of Octavia Butler give an African-American dimension to the art of science-fiction writing, and the sure, joyous voice of the late poet and writer Audre Lorde to document the beauty and courage that accompanies lesbian love.

Few extraordinary Black women in the arts have broken through the barriers of Hollywood over the past twenty-five years to make an impact in the mediums of motion pictures and television. A major breakthrough of this era, however, came with *Lady Sings the Blues*, the 1972 film that brought Diana Ross to the big screen, and cast for one of the rare times in American film history a Black woman in a leading-lady role that exuded glamour, style, and human complexity. It also brought a big-screen, Black love story into our hearts and gave us a Black matinee idol, Billy Dee Williams, who would portray the strength and beauty of the Black man with power and dignity.

The film became the seminal turning point that would open the door to

CLOCKWISE FROM RIGHT:
Diana Ross and her 20 years of song and style were celebrated with a holiday cover story.
December 1980
Photo, Rolf Bruderer

Whoopi Goldberg's one-woman Broadway show combined controversial social commentary and humor.
March 1985
Photo, Darius Anthony

Pulitzer prize-winner Alice Walker won international praise for such works as The Color Purple *and* Possessing the Secret of Joy.
September 1989
Photo, Dwight Carter

Cicely Tyson, one of the nation's finest actresses, after her starring role in Sounder, *which earned her an Academy Award nomination.*
February 1973
Photo, Si Chi Ko

Diana Sands reflected on her art in an early Essence *interview.*
August 1970
Photo, Howard Simmons

Hollywood for a greater number and more diverse mix of Black actresses, beginning with Cicely Tyson, who brought epic majesty to her stunning roles in the film *Sounder* (1972), and the television miniseries, "A Woman Called Moses" (1978). The incomparable Diahann Carroll paved the way for Black women in television with her hit series "Julia" in the late sixties through early seventies, and made the ordinary life of a Black woman nothing less than heroic in the 1974 film *Claudine*. But it took Whoopi Goldberg, with her Oscar-winning performance in the film *Ghost*, and her nineties *Sister Act* hits to prove that the natural, African beauty of Black women can be highly bankable in Hollywood.

Just as significant during this time has been the emergence of Black women behind the camera in the motion picture industry. Suzanne de Passe, formerly president of Motown Productions and now head of her own de Passe Entertainment, became a Hollywood mogul in the truest sense of the word, with a track record of award-winning television hits ("Motown 25: Yesterday, Today, Forever," "Lonesome Dove," "The Jacksons: An American Family Dream," "Small Sacrifices") to prove she not only knows what sells but knows what is good. She also received an Oscar nomination for writing the screenplay of *Lady Sings the Blues*.

Others who have attained power in Hollywood during the last two and one-half decades include manager Dolores Robinson, whose roster of clients have included both Blacks and Whites, from Wesley Snipes to Martin Sheen; and television screenwriter and producer Winifred Hervey, who wrote Emmy-winning scripts for the comedy series "The Golden Girls" in the eighties, and served as executive producer for the popular urban-hip television show "The Fresh Prince of Bel Air" in the early nineties. Never in our history have Black women been in such supply at the tables of power in Hollywood—the industry that so commandingly sets the standard for the images we come to internalize.

One media personality would come to emerge at the end of the eighties,

Singer-actress Diahann Carroll was the first Black woman to have her own television sitcom, "Julia." Throughout her impressive career she has symbolized grace, style, and timeless beauty.
October 1984
Photo, Bobby Holland

however, with cosmic power extending into the final decade of the century and a trajectory of popular success that seems infinite. She would recreate the standards and defy all the odds to become the single most beloved television personality of her time. She is Oprah Winfrey, the multiple Emmy Award-winning daytime-television talk-show host, Academy Award-nominated film actress, television producer, and studio owner, who became the highest paid woman in the entertainment industry in 1993. She has come to define the very essence of Black Power in America at the end of the century: rich, revered, respected, and our best living proof that within each of us resides the power for self-actualization.

If it has only been in the last twenty-five years that Hollywood started showcasing the talents of Black women in fuller-dimensioned, more positive roles, the music and recording industry has had a considerably longer tradition of affirming our talents. Indeed, we entered the seventies on the names of some Black female singers whose artistry extended back to the sixties and was of such enduring excellence that it insured their popularity through the rest of the century: Nancy Wilson, Aretha Franklin, and Tina Turner have all celebrated thirty-year anniversaries in the recording industry and have found a new legion of fans with each succeeding generation. They have been the standard bearers paving the way for a new crop of torch singers who would similarly mark the eighties and nineties.

Fifty albums later, grand diva and song stylist Nancy Wilson.
October 1986
Photo, Bobby Holland

Natalie Cole and Whitney Houston are two who not only followed these divas, but who have followed in the tradition of their respective families. Natalie Cole, heir to the rich legacy of her father Nat "King" Cole, evoked the power of ancestors with her colossal *Unforgettable* album, a superb orchestration of technology that joined her singing with that of her late father's,

Best-selling singer and tremendous talent Whitney Houston.
December 1990
Photo, Ken Nahoum

and which won six Grammy Awards in 1991. Two years later, Whitney Houston, daughter of soul singer Cissy Houston and first cousin of popular songstress Dionne Warwick, walked away with a Grammy Award for virtually every category in which she and her mega album, *The Bodyguard*, were nominated. And singer Janet Jackson, the cute kid actress who appeared on television's "Good Times" during the seventies, would prove during the eighties and nineties that she was more than Michael Jackson's baby sister, but a phenom in her own right.

During the last twenty-five years we've also witnessed the prominence and success of Black women as leading performers in opera, with Leontyne Price, Jessye Norman, and Kathleen Battle being major contributors. These and other classical vocal artists have achieved international acclaim and set the standard for operatic mastery.

Showstopper Anna Maria Horsford won our hearts as Thelma on television's "Amen."
July 1987
Photo, Cynthia Moore

There are also now Black women in the executive suites of record companies. One of them, Sylvia Rhone, is chairman and CEO of Elektra Entertainment Group and EastWest Records. And Black women have clearly had an impact on the male-dominated hip-hop music culture that marked the nineties. Witness the reign of Queen Latifah, the hip-hop star who is not only a successful rap artist, but a consummate businesswoman who runs her own record company, as CEO of Flavor Unit Records and Management, which also manages the careers of other rappers. Latifah is one of the few entertainers who also successfully made the move from recording artist to television star. Her hit sitcom "Living Single," which debuted in 1993, features an ensemble cast of Black actresses living out the foibles and fantasies of the contemporary Black woman. The crossover appeal of the show again speaks to the enduring popularity of the richly textured Black female experience.

If our celebrity stars have shone brightly these past twenty-five years, so too has the brilliance of activists in our community been a continuing source of inspirational light and leadership. In 1987, *Essence* magazine launched the annual Essence Awards which have included honors to women-activists in our community whose labor and love have helped to make the community measurably better. One of the first Essence Awards went to Georgette Watson, a dynamic woman from Boston who risked her life to run the anti-drug program she conceived and launched in the city's drug-plagued Roxbury section. Numerous convictions for drug offenses resulted from the first year of her Drop-a-Dime community drug-busting program.

Janet Jackson grew from the sassy little sister on television to a singing superstar.
May 1993
Photo, Yuri Elizondo

As is often the case with lives that are lived on a heroic scale, many of our community activists have become celebrities in their own right—their works being of such magnitude and significance that the public at large is forced to take note and give due. One of the most dedicated and respected in that league is the crusader for children, Marian Wright Edelman, whose Children's Defense Fund has become the most powerful voice in the country speaking out on behalf of children. Since founding the CDF in 1973, Edelman has earned the ear of both presidents and parents alike, and the undying love of the children whose issues she so valiantly champions.

Chicago educator Marva Collins, who left the public school system twenty years ago to begin the Westside Preparatory School, continually proves that even "disadvantaged" children are ripe for academic excellence if encouraged, supported, and respected. And Black women from and of the community, such as Bertha Gilkey in St. Louis, who pioneered the concept of tenants managing the housing projects they live in; and "Sweet Alice" Harris in Los Angeles, who proved that even the seemingly "hardcore unemployable" can learn to work with pride and dignity, are brilliant testaments to the awesome power of community activism at the grassroots level. From Fannie Lou Hamer to Lani Guinier or Rosa Parks to Sister Souljah, activism among Black women may take diverse shapes and styles, but at its heart has always been the singular commitment to moving the lives of Black folks forward.

The level of personal best that Black women bring to the arena of physical competition has always been evident in the field of sports, whether it was Althea Gibson turning tennis on its ear in 1957 and 1958 by winning two Wimbledon championships, or Wilma Rudolph, who would overcome the effects of polio and go on to spectacularly win three gold medals in track events during the 1960 Olympics in Rome. Like their Black male counterparts, Black women tend to dominate in track and field in international competitions and have made the crucial difference to the United States bringing home the gold in Olympic competitions over the past two decades. We watched spellbound as sprinter Evelyn Ashford dashed across the finish line in the 1984 Olympics to win the gold medal in the 100 meters, setting a new Olympic record. We watched the famed sisters-in-law Jackie Joyner-Kersee and Florence Griffith Joyner become the darlings of the 1988 and 1992 Olympics. Flo-Jo won three gold medals for track in 1988 (100 and 200 meters and 100-meter relay) and Jackie returned in 1992 to add to her 1988 gold medal wins in the heptathlon (a two-day, seven-event competition that includes running and javelin throwing) and the long jump competitions by winning another gold and a bronze medal.

That year we also watched Gail Devers win the gold medal in a thrilling 100-meter dash—thrilling because she had overcome Graves' disease and the near amputation of her feet to make her run to victory.

Black female athletes during the last twenty-five years have proven to be much more than runners and jumpers, however. Anita De Frantz, for example, was a member of the U.S. Women's Rowing Team that took the bronze medal in the 1976 Olympics. She went on to further distinction by becoming the first African-American elected to the International Olympic Committee in 1986. Ice skaters Tai Babilonia and Debbi Thomas brought grace and beauty to the 1980 and 1988 winter Olympics, respectively, while fencer Sharon Monplaisir and equestrian Melanie Wright gave African-American style to two ancient European arts. And Zina Garrison became the second Black female tennis player after Althea Gibson to compete in the Wimbledon finals in 1990.

Win or lose, our athletes, like Black women in all other arenas of endeavor over the past two and one-half decades, mark the rise of what can be considered a true championship season.

OPPOSITE:
The woman behind the medals: Olympic athlete Jackie Joyner-Kersee.
August 1989
Photo, Dwight Carter

Four gold medals later, Olympic athlete Florence Griffith Joyner.
March 1989
Photo, Dwight Carter

TOP ROW:

The original "every-woman," singer Chaka Khan is a soulful siren.
January 1986
Photo, Gregory Kent

Singer-activist Miriam Makeba brought the struggle in South Africa home to African-Americans.
March 1988
Photo, William Coupon

Syncopated and sassy: veteran jazz singer Carmen McRae.
October 1986
Photo, Bobby Holland

MIDDLE ROW:

Legendary singer Betty "Bebop" Carter.
December 1983
Photo, Bobby Holland

Nina Simone, pianist, composer, and vocalist wooed the world with her unique, beautiful style.
October 1985
Photo, Dwight Carter

Blues singer, Alberta Hunter, remained popular for over five decades, with some of her greatest fame coming when she was in her 80s.
October 1978
Photo, Seiji Kakizaki

BOTTOM ROW:

Toni Braxton, a classic chanteuse.
December 1993
Photo, Daniela Federici/LaFace Records

The premier gospel singer, Mahalia Jackson.
December 1970
Photo, A.P. Worldwide

Singer, composer, pianist, Roberta Flack.
December 1982
Photo, Francesco Scavullo

FAR LEFT:

The talented Queen of the Blues, Dinah Washington, died 20 years before this photo appeared in print.
May 1983
Photo, courtesy of the Astor, Lenox and Tilden Foundations at the Schomburg Center for Research in Black Culture, New York Public Library

NEAR LEFT:

Tina Turner: proud, independent, and free spirited.
July 1993
Photo, Nicola Dill

Singer, actress, and Broadway star Melba Moore.
April 1988
Photo, Enrique Badulescu

I am reminded of a Senegalese proverb that says: "If a centipede loses a leg, it does not prevent it from walking." Historically and today, we African-American women face continuous efforts to stop us from moving forward. But Black women are determined to make do when don't tries to prevail.

When you are both Black and female, from the days when you are a very small child you keep hearing two awful words, "You can't! You can't learn complicated things like science—that's for white kids. You shouldn't worry yourself with math—girls don't like math. You better settle for a job cleaning up airplane cabins—after all who ever heard of a Black woman pilot?"

My sisters refuse to build their lives around I can't. Throughout history, countless African-American women have refused to live by these words. How well Black women know the bitter stings of racism and sexism; and so many of our sisters are also assaulted by merciless poverty. But through their extraordinary strength, determination, and faith, at some point in her life, every Black woman says I can!

—Johnetta B. Cole, July 1994

What resonates for me is that we not see ourselves as victims—that we not see ourselves as without any control over important decisions in our lives. We are survivors, not victims, and we have to take a stand or take a step or make a statement that allows us to move from being the victim of other people's decisions to the architect of our own well-being and that of our community and country.

—Lani Guinier, "Challenging Power"
by Audrey Edwards and Susan L. Taylor, October 1994

My extraordinary parents were the best human beings; they were proud and patriotic Americans and they were the embodiment of strong and courageous womanhood and manhood. They were and continue to be my greatest inspiration.

They taught me and my brother how blessed we are to be born Americans where opportunities are abundant. They instilled in us the desire and drive to be the best at our chosen goals and although our paths may prove difficult at times, to accept the challenges and remember that accomplishments have no color; that a mountain can never be climbed successfully looking down. The direction should always be onward and upward, and with faith, focus, discipline, dedication and hard work, our dreams will be realized.

—Leontyne Price, August 1994

Fresh from the film
Malcolm X, *actress Angela Bassett was the leading lady for a holiday cover story.*
December 1992
Photo, George Holz

Gladys Knight, after almost 40 years in show business.
October 1991
Photo, Randee St. Nicholas

BOTTOM LEFT:
Downhome diva Patti LaBelle.
March 1991
Photo, Kaz Chiba

BOTTOM RIGHT:
Dianne Reeves's self-titled debut album topped the jazz charts for 11 weeks in the 1980s.
January 1989
Photo, Enrique Badulescu

OPPOSITE:
Singer Jody Watley basks in the glamour of her 1988 Grammy Award for Best New Artist.
May 1988
Photo, Buckmaster

My daughter was on her way to see me one day, when she happened to pass a woman sitting on the street, holding her sleeping baby. The woman, an addict, was nodding, and the baby kept slipping out of her hands.

Lorraine walked away, but then turned around, thinking, "We're not doing anything, we're just talking about these things, you know, we see it and we walk away . . . if nobody does anything, this is another generation down the drain."

So, she went back to the woman and said, "You need a little help with the baby. My mother has always taken care of children and will be glad to help you. She's lived here on this block for thirty years, you can ask anybody about her. Bring the baby, you don't have to sign any papers or sign your life away, and you don't have to give us any money. Just bring the baby and let us take care of it until you get yourself together. The only thing that we ask of you is that you go on a drug program and try to be a woman—you know, get off of it."

My daughter even forgot to tell me about it, but sure enough, the next day, I saw this addict standing at the door with her baby. I got on the phone to Lorraine and asked, "Did you send an addict here?" She said, "Well, it's just a baby, you know—to take care of." I decided o.k., I took the baby and kept her.

—Clara Hale, "Hale House" by Frances E. Ruffin, July 1972

FAR LEFT:
A sultry Stephanie Mills proved she was no longer Dorothy from Oz with the release of If I Were Your Woman in the 1980s.
January 1988
Photo, Buckmaster

NEAR LEFT:
Grammy Award-winning songstress Anita Baker.
December 1987
Photo, Buckmaster

CLOCKWISE, FROM THE TOP:

Alfre Woodard, an actress of immense style and talent.
May 1994
Photo, David Roth

From "Nothing But A Man" to "For the Love of Ivy," actress-singer Abbey Lincoln has always performed songs her own way.
April 1992
Photo, Frank Ockenfels 3/Outline

Debbie Allen, the brilliant dancer, choreographer, and director.
June 1990
Photo, Frank Maresca

Jackée was introduced to television audiences on the popular "227."
May 1992
Photo, Roger Neve

*Billie Holiday's voice
captured our beauty and
our pain.
June 1981
Photo, Frank Driggs
Collection; illustration by
Richie Williamson*

Then, there was little Hattie McDaniel. When I got out to Hollywood and this great schism—this great isolation—was being created between me and other Black actors, Miss McDaniel sent for me. That's when I found out what a grande dame she was. She told me, "I wear two hats too. I've had to. I make money, and I take care of my relatives. Our people give me hell, and so do white folks. We're strong and we do what we have to. You're not to be unhappy about it. You're not to cry about it." She spoke with the same will and authority my grandmother had. Miss McDaniel said, "This is not the way I am, but they don't want me the way I am. So I put my handkerchief on and I am the best mammy that they've ever seen, and when I come home I take that handkerchief off."

She was a queen. I was so lucky that she brought me to see her.

—Lena Horne, "Lena!" by Audreen Buffalo, May 1985

OPPOSITE:

*The legendary Lena Horne
in the 15th anniversary
issue.
May 1985
Photo, Gerard Gentil*

My undying love and respect goes to those extraordinary unknown lost women I searched for in my mother and father's past, who escaped and survived famine, floods, fires, invasions, earthquakes, slavery and epidemics long enough to create my precious sisters and myself. I rejoice in the circle of their loving spirits. And the beat goes on and on and on.

—Carmen Delavallade, August 1994

ABOVE:

Dr. Mae Jemison, the first Black female astronaut, was interviewed in Essence *by Nikki Giovanni, who shared the nation's enthusiasm for this incredible woman.*
April 1993
Photo, Chris Callis

ABOVE LEFT:

As a dancer and later as artistic director of the Alvin Ailey Dance Company, Judith Jamison captures the movement of a people.
May 1985
Photo, Jack Mitchell

At 17, Olympic-hopeful Stacey Gunthorpe ranked as the country's seventh best gymnast.
September 1988
Photo, Jenafer Gillingham

*Artist, activist, author,
Samella Lewis was editor of*
Black Art *magazine and
founder of the Museum of
African-American Art in
Los Angeles.*
May 1990
Photo, N. Stephen Chin

*Angela Davis, a legendary
activist.*
August 1986
Photo, Gregory Kent

*Filmmaker Julie Dash
captured the Gullah women
of South Carolina in her
visually stunning film*
Daughters of the Dust.
October 1989
Photo, N. Stephen Chin

*Annette Samuels, Essence's
first fashion editor and a
former secretary to President
Jimmy Carter, graced a
feature on being fine,
fabulous, and over 40.*
May 1982
Photo, Francesco Scavullo

*In a candid interview, Dr.
Betty Shabazz shared her
memories of her late
husband in "Loving and
Losing Malcolm."*
February 1992
Photo, Anthony Mills

*Marta Moreno Vega
founded New York City's
Caribbean Cultural Center
to reunite Black people
worldwide.*
May 1990
Photo, Brad Guice

OPPOSITE:

*Long live the Queen:
Latifah (aka Dana Owens)
heads her own
entertainment empire.
October 1993
Photo, Timothy White*

*An international star of the
1920s, Josephine Baker was
loved by the world for her
daring style and generous
spirit.
February 1991
Photo, courtesy of
Schomburg Center for
Research in Black Culture,
New York Public Library*

*Sweet Honey in the Rock's
lush harmonies and
powerful lyrics continue to
thrill and enlighten
listeners.
May 1987
Photo, Dwight Carter*

123

The ever-resilient Winnie Mandela was among the first Black women to assume power in the parliament of the new South Africa.
April 1994
Photo, Peter Magubane/ Gamma Liaison

I am deeply gratified that my community, the Black people, though taken aback by my woman-centeredness at the beginning of my career has hung in there with me for twenty-five years, learning, as I have, that we still have a whole lot more to do and to say. Not infrequently the scope of our tasks, as artists, mothers, 'race-women' is overwhelming; my instincts have been to tackle one issue from as many angles as I possibly can. Sometimes, this focus lends itself to misinterpretations, to false accusations of treachery and lack of vision. I know this for a fact. Yet, Black women have not been intimidated by voices seeking to minimize, trivialize, or banish our very real dilemmas from discussion or action in the public domain. From Single Black Mothers, Inc. to Alpha Kappa Alpha, we've determined that no kinds of chains, psychological or socio-economic, are gonna defeat us.

—Ntozake Shange, July 1994

Choice is the essence of freedom. The freedom to choose one's destiny, free of persecution, is the driving force of all human rights movements. African-Americans have struggled since slavery to control our lives—the right to decide where we want to sit on a bus, the right to vote. That women can be singled out for the denial of the power to control our most personal decisions is unacceptable in a civilized world. It is immoral and inhuman to coerce the childbearing decisions of any individual.

It would have been impossible to lead a movement engaged in one of the most contentious issues of our time had I not been the daughter of and raised among those of uncommon courage—the courage to stand against intolerance and aggression against women. My passion in defense of women's rights to self-determination was formed in the crucible of an early career in nursing, where I saw first-hand the burden of illegal birth control and abortion borne on the bodies of poor women. This usually meant women of color.

Social progress comes about through the sustained dedication to creating better prospects for the human condition. It is rarely achieved through occasional involvement. If my life and work have inspired other women to seize the power within themselves to securing a future for our daughters, free of coercion or limitation because of their gender, I will consider the challenge of the battle as having been worth it.

—Faye Wattleton, August 1994

Some folks think that writing is scary. It often is. But I'm willing to make the emotional investment because when I was growing up, my mama taught me that anything worth doing in life should be a little scary, that you have to be willing to jump off the cliff before you can see where you might land; but you have to believe that you're going to land. So my investment is an emotional one, and it is expensive, but I'm willing to pay, because sometimes it's inside that so-called danger zone that I discover where the secrets of happiness are hiding.

—Terry McMillan, "The Love We've Lost," May 1993

Our Beauty

"**B**lack is Beautiful!" The words rose like a war chant to become our mantra, our anthem—and the rallying cry that signaled not just a new era but a new ethos. Indeed, the single most defining feature of the civil rights and women's movements has not necessarily been the great leap forward taken in the political and social and economic spheres of Black life during the last twenty-five years, but may instead be the sweeping psychological revolution that occurred regarding our vision of ourselves. Our standards and perceptions of beauty were so radically altered during this time that the very label *Black*—once considered an insulting pejorative—became the very designation by which we would call, identify, and affirm ourselves. It was a shift of seismic proportions that marked a new Black consciousness.

Essence captured this emerging sensibility with the cover of its first issue in May 1970 that showed a full-featured, bronze-colored beauty coming out of shadow to face the dawn of a brighter day. Framing her face like a halo was glistening natural hair, which, perhaps more than any other physical attribute of the time, defined the essence of Black beauty.

By whatever name we chose to call the style—the "natural," the "Afro," the "fro," or the "bush"—we entered the seventies reveling in the crowning glory of "unprocessed" Black hair. For the first time in our history in America, our God-given hair, with all of its rich textures of hard and soft waves, curls, and kinks, would be worn in its natural state with pride and even a touch of defiance.

What would mark this era was the extent to which Black hair became political, a measure of one's Blackness or political correctness. Yet for the Black woman, the last twenty-five years has also meant the liberating freedom to wear hair kinky or straight, to wear cornrows or dreadlocks, weaves or wigs, to be braided or clean shaven. Indeed, what we've come to understand and appreciate is that the real beauty of Black hair lies in its enormous versatility. It can be shaped, sculpted, and styled in an almost infinite variety of looks—picked into standing up straight, pressed or permed into lying down flat, twisted into corkscrews, carved into words. No other group of women have more options than do Black women when it comes to wearing hair.

And no other magazine has showcased the splendid spectrum of Black hair styles with more love and respect than *Essence* during these last twenty-five years—and in the process helped establish the reputations of some Black women who virtually became known by their hair. The model Pat Evans, whose perfectly-

Wearing a natural crown,
supermodel Roshumba.
May 1990
Photo, Kaz Chiba

Bold and beautiful: cutting it close.
September 1993
Photo, John Peden

shaped, clean-shaven head became her signature look in the seventies, came to define the very essence of haute couture. Singer Roberta Flack's enormous Afro gave her queenly demeanor natural majesty, while Nina Simone's regal cornrows helped crown her the empress of soul. Model Norma Jean Darden allowed us to count the ways we could wear our hair naturally. And by the nineties, Oscar-winning actress Whoopi Goldberg had long donned dreadlocks.

Hair, however, was only the tip of the revolution in Black beauty and perceptions of beauty that marked the past couple of decades. The African-American beauty of Black women became recognized in the one event that has traditionally set the national standard for *all*-American beauty: the Miss America Pageant. Vanessa Williams was the first Black woman crowned Miss America in 1984, and during the next ten years, four more Black women would wear the crown, and thus permanently alter a society's definition of beauty.

During this period, the voluptuous full-figured Black woman became a new feminine standard, due almost single-handedly to *Essence*, which was the first publication to regularly feature our full, vital form in its fashion and other editorial pages. The first national magazine cover that Oprah Winfrey ever graced was *Essence*—when she was still a large-sized personality. And when the models Peggy Dillard and Phyllis Cuington ripened in the eighties to the fuller bloom of beauty, they were in even greater demand as models for fashion and beauty layouts in the magazine.

Of course, the real standard for beauty during the last twenty-five years came to be measured by health and fitness. And again *Essence* has been on the forefront documenting the importance of good physical health over pounds and dress size. It was in *Essence* that we learned a size 16 is no less beautiful than a size 6 if the body is healthy—if one eats right, properly exercises, and feels good about herself. It was in *Essence* that we learned to love our big legs, our round behinds, our full hips, and our rich variety of Black selves.

We also learned how to enhance our natural good looks through the art of make-up specifically geared to us. We learned to use henna extracts from Africa to color our hair and kohl colors to highlight our eyes.

Actress Joie Lee.
February 1988
Photo, David Lee

Ta-ning.
April 1993
Photo, Matthew Jordan
Smith

Naomi Campbell.
April 1991
Photo, Kip Meyer

Also during this time, Black women have become the latest audience pursued by manufacturers. Cosmetic giants such as Maybelline, Revlon, Clairol, and L'Oréal now carry make-up, skin care, and hair product lines targeted to Black women. And just as significantly, cosmetic manufacturers have signed Black models into the sphere of "supermodel." Veronica Webb, Tyra Banks, Naomi Campbell, Beverly Johnson, and Iman have all become famous not just for their glorious faces and forms, but for the products they pitch.

Black businesses catering to our special health and beauty needs have also taken root and blossomed since the seventies, growing beyond our traditional barbershops and Black beauty parlors to become hair salons, or Black-owned salons offering a range of services from pedicures to herbal body wraps. Names such as Johnson Products and Fashion Fair became household words in an age that witnessed the beauty of the Black market and realized its great profits. All of which confirms what we discovered at the dawn of our new age: Black *is* truly beautiful.

Beverly Johnson and Ann Fowler with hair pulled-back for timeless beauty.
September 1970
Photo, Larry Couzens

NEAR RIGHT:

A natural beauty.
June 1987
Photo, Dwight Carter

FAR RIGHT:

Ms. Olympia 1983, Carla Dunlap: a portrait of upper-body strength.
October 1985
Photo, Paul B. Goode

TOP LEFT:

*Sister and brother Megen
and Mario Van Peebles in
hair designer James
Finney's plaits.
July 1981
Photo, Michel Momy*

TOP RIGHT:

*Cornrows adorned.
July 1981
Photo, Michel Momy*

*Dancer Dyane Harvey-
Salaam.
May 1990
Photo, Kaz Chiba*

OPPOSITE:

*Braids that go on . . .
January 1994
Photo, John Peden*

Setting the style with a curly perm.
February 1984
Photo, Nesti

BOTTOM LEFT:
Andre Douglas introduces his new line, It's A Wig.
May 1978
Photo, John Galluzzi

BOTTOM RIGHT:
The layered bob for spring.
April 1989
Photo, Tom Wool

OPPOSITE:
One mo' time: retro beauty from the 1970s.
August 1970
Photo, Saul Leiter

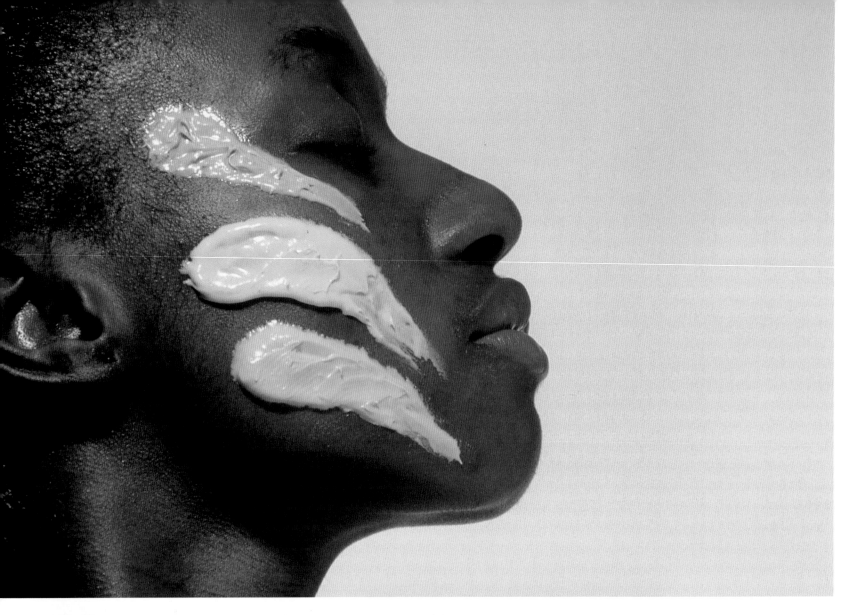

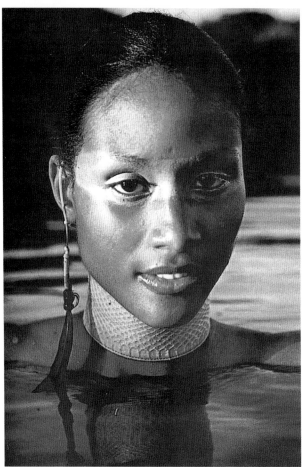

Essence shares secrets of maintaining great beauty with the latest products.
February 1990
Photo, Todd Gray

FAR LEFT:

Beverly Johnson, four years before she was the first Black model to appear on the cover of Vogue.
September 1970
Photo, Chris Von Wangenheim

NEAR LEFT:

Top model Billie Blair wears Alexis Kirk's pewter choker with ivory pendants and four-horn necklace.
November 1972
Photo, Ken Mori

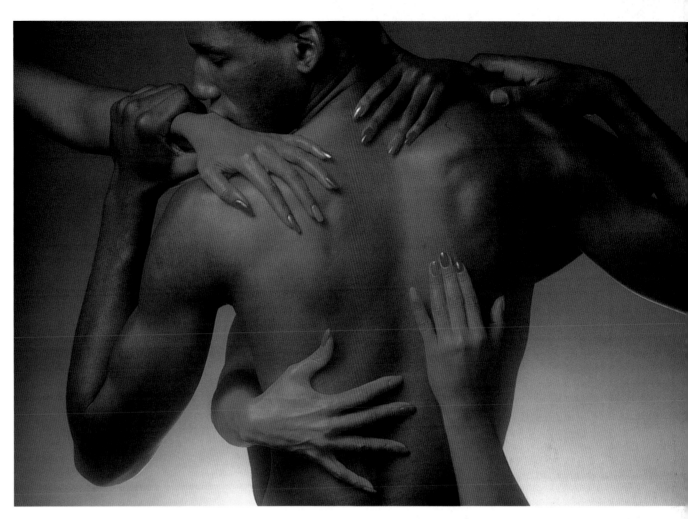

January 1975
Photo, Ken Mori

Tyra Banks.
June 1993
Photo, Mark Baptiste

139

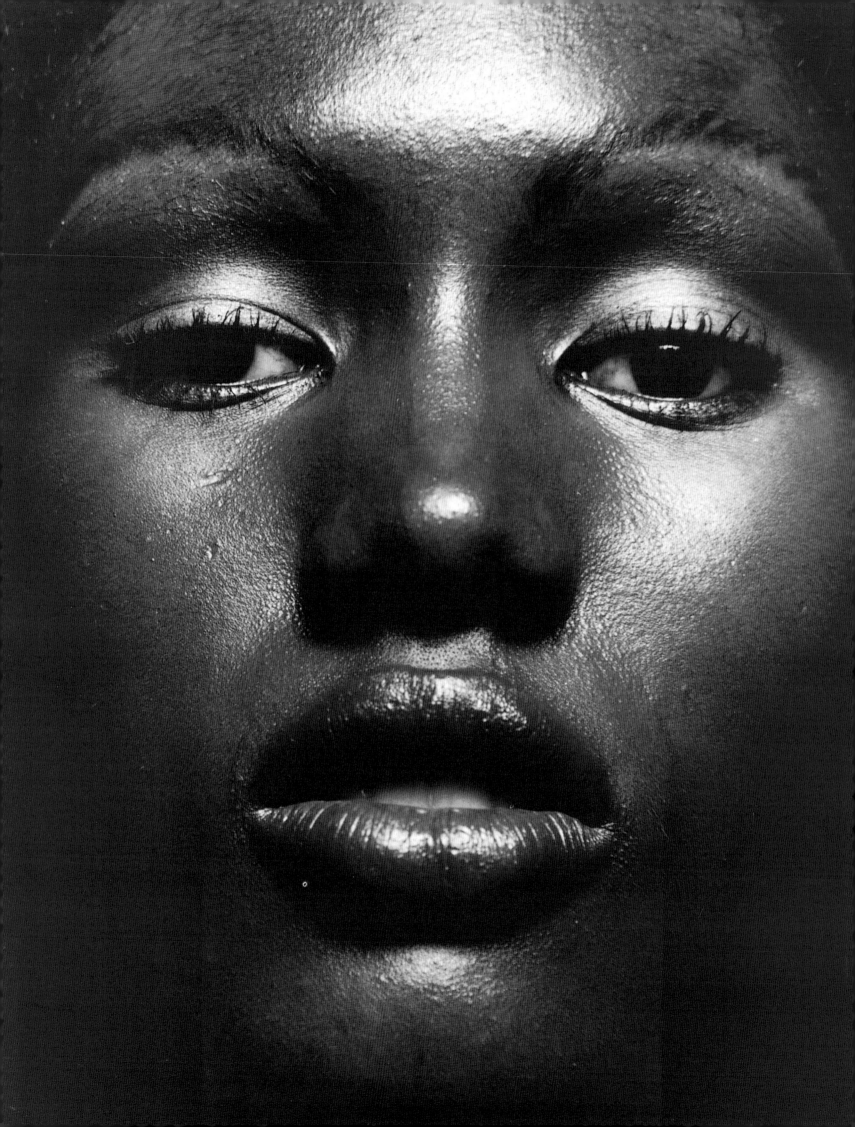

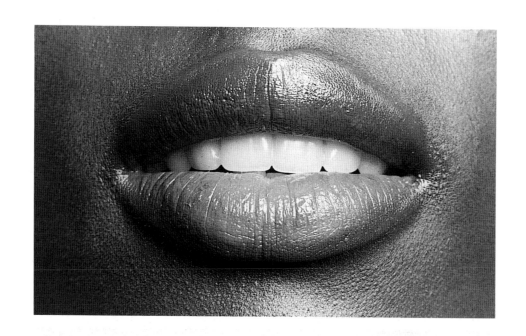

OPPOSITE:

Grace Jones, full face.
October 1971
Photo, Anthony Barboza

TOP:

The beautiful lips of Grace
Jones.
March 1971
Photo, Larry Couzens

BOTTOM:

Fresh, uncomplicated style.
October 1988
Photo, Buckmaster

January 1988
Photo, Jon Goossens

OPPOSITE:

Comedian and actress
Phyllis Yvonne Stickney.
October 1986
Photo, Isabel Snyder

In a way I feel we're pleasing everyone but ourselves. We know what we respond to and what we venerate, but if we don't watch it, in a while we won't be able to remember. Part of our legacy is to maintain these values so that our children will be able to see the beauty of their ancestors' faces. I want very much to tend that responsibility so that our cultural and value base is preserved.

We must first of all really love ourselves—what we have done and what we have been. I don't mean pretend to love it cause pretend love is crappy; it will get you absolutely nowhere. But the things that we do love we really have to fight for. Whatever stems from true love of self, of what our ancestors have been, will be good for us and a fine legacy.

—Alice Walker, "An Interview with Alice Walker" by Jessica Harris, July 1976

I rejoice in twenty-five years of absorbing the explosion of information and knowledge about pre-colonial Africa, pre-chattel slavery, African people, and the glory of majesty of ancient Kemetic Kingdoms.

I rejoice in the genius of our immediate ancestors who fanned the dim flame of hope and whispered messages of promise and glory through spirituals, in dance, in shouts, and in the beat of the drums. I rejoice in the foresight of our intellectual giants who brought the truths of "our story" and placed our faces on the map of human history. I discern the impact of their truth by the venomous nature of the attacks against their scholarship, their orality, and their passionate persistence. It was these men: Dr. John H. Clarke, Dr. Yosef Ben-Jochannan, Dr. Molefi K. Asante, Dr. Asa Hilliard, Dr. Wade Noble, Dr. Jacob Carruthers, and Dr. Maulana Karenga along with others who brought to us sisters the Isis principle; the reign of Hatshepsut, the healing qualities of Hathor, the courage of Makeda, and the endurance of the Orishas.

I rejoice in African women emerging, looking back to move forward, peeling off the layers of postured encapsulation in which we encased ourselves protectively from the fangs of rape, ravish, and abuse which denied our loveliness— tenuous, but determined, reclaiming our destiny. Isis-like, we search for the pieces of the dismembered body of the African man—scattered awry. We wash the broken fragments with our tears, willing their healing, loving every tortured fragment.

We dare to give birth to sons and daughters—they who will build families and nations worthy of their creator and of their ancestors. We prepare them in their childhood sweetness to know who they are, to assess the circumstances of their existence, to identify and analyze the face of the historical oppressor, to recognize the multiplicity of masks he wears and the varied array of garish tools he employs. We pluck and scour the foul debris from their bodies and spirits as they navigate America's sewers—these "ghettos" that have been created by others but are labeled "our community." We love our children profoundly with a love that embraces, protects, and emboldens them though time and space and physical death may separate us.

I rejoice in my certainty that we will not give up. We are vital, sagacious, and grounded. We will persist—as long as flowers grow, as long as blossoms become fruit and caterpillars turn into butterflies, as long as the ocean tides respond to the pull of the moon, as long as birds sing and nest and fly, as long as fish swim, as long as rivers flow, as long as mating consummates, as long as love lasts. May the ancestors rejoice in our work.

—Adelaide L. Sanford, August 1994

Naomi Campbell became one of the top international models by the early 1990s.
October 1987
Photo, Gerard Gentil

FAR LEFT:
Model Amalia in the autumn blush.
September 1982
Photo, Jacques Malignon

January 1983
Photo, Rolf Bruderer

OPPOSITE:
Wanakee.
September 1984
Photo, John Peden

Identical twin models
Dortensia and Lortensia.
December 1988
Photo, Buckmaster

Cherchez la femme:
Beauties in Paris.
October 1987
Photos, Gerard Gentil

The sheer power, God-given grace, potential, peace, good health, and unrelentless beauty is the legacy of us all, Black women.

—Naomi Sims, July 1994

Supermodel Naomi Sims
changed the face of
American beauty.
January 1988
Photo, Tom Wool

LEFT:

Vanessa Williams, the first Black woman to be crowned Miss America, has achieved success as a recording artist and Broadway star.
August 1994
Photo, Matthew Jordan Smith

OPPOSITE ABOVE:

Marjorie Judith Vincent, Miss America 1991, went on to become a lawyer and a TV news anchor.
January 1991
Photo, Ken Nahoum

OPPOSITE BELOW:

Debbye Turner, 1990 Miss America, now a veterinarian.
January 1990
Photo, Dwight Carter

Models Barbara Smith, now owner of B. Smith's Restaurants in New York City and Washington, D.C., and Ben Lawson in the Caribbean.
April 1983
Photo, Frank Schramm

November 1983
Photo, John Pinderhughes

BOTTOM LEFT:
Quiet time for intimacy.
May 1981
Photo, Gerard Gentil

BOTTOM RIGHT:
Iman in Jamaica. Who are
you, Rasta man?
July 1980
Photo, Mel Dixon

Cynthia Miller—from the
20th Anniversary Cover
issue.
May 1990
Photo, David Roth

BOTTOM LEFT:
The workout: beauty and
the body.
June 1988
Photo, Buckmaster

BOTTOM RIGHT:
The luscious lips of model
and former Miss Jamaica,
Althea Laing.
May 1990
Photo, Kaz Chiba

OPPOSITE:
The beauty of bronze.
May 1990
Photo, Kaz Chiba

Our Spiritual Connections

If the civil rights and women's rights movements of the last twenty-five years transformed the aspirations of Black women, that transformation was nowhere more keenly felt than in our personal relationships—with our men, with other women, with the larger society. And with our Higher Being.

The empowered, liberated Black woman who began to emerge in the seventies came full blown into the "transitional" age of changing roles and rising expectations that marked the eighties and nineties. It was a time that introduced us to the concepts of the superwoman and the liberated man; of women who could have it all and men who could learn to get in touch with their feelings. It was a time that also tested the Black family, strained the ties between Black men and women, and bestowed options that would result in greater opportunities, some of which also led to greater uncertainty.

At the dawn of the seventies, however, a certain romanticism still fueled the expectations of civil rights that would spill over into interpersonal relationships. The traditional notions that accompanied "man and woman" were being replaced by the revolutionary, communal idealogy of "brother and sister." Black men became "warriors" in the struggle for civil rights and women their beautiful "queens."

By the mid-seventies, the revolutionary power of Black women had become a decisive factor in the urban guerrilla Black Power movement that defined much of the civil rights struggle in America's northern cities, most notably in California, the golden state that has given us Hollywood, Disneyland, and a certain enduring romantic optimism. It was in Northern California, particularly the Bay Area with its sizeable Black population and revolutionary fervor, that the passions of politics became stoked by the passions of love. The women of the Black Power era who captured our attention and entered the public consciousness were invariably linked not just to the revolution, but to the revolutionary Black men they dared to love. Angela Davis, who loved George Jackson, faced the charges and stood trial when she was accused of being the mastermind behind the bold attempted prison break that resulted in Jonathan Jackson, George's brother, being killed in 1970. Elaine Brown, who loved Huey Newton, took command of the Black Panther Party when he faced murder charges and fled the country in 1974.

Angela Davis, the symbol of political activism, was offered bail by Aretha Franklin during the "Free Angela" campaign of the early 1970s.
August 1981
Photo, Hilton Braithwaite

The joy of sisterhood in Barbados.
May 1988
Photo, Enrique Badulescu

Kathleen Cleaver, who loved Eldridge Cleaver, stood by her man through all the personal and political struggles that marked their "movement marriage." Through these women we learned that Black love is not only a political act requiring great commitment that can exact a great cost, but that such love also possesses its own revolutionary magic.

As the decade of the seventies drew to an end, however, the romance of Black love and revolutionary magic began to lose much of its luster. In 1979, twenty-seven-year-old Black feminist Michele Wallace's provocative book *Black Macho and the Myth of the Superwoman* was published and set the stage for skirmishes, wars, and rumors of war that were to ignite relationships between Black men and women for the rest of the century. Four years earlier another young Black woman—a playwright named Ntozake Shange—had drawn first blood with her incendiary work *For Colored Girls Who Have Considered Suicide When the Rainbow is Enuf*. Wallace and Shange marked the ascendancy of a new Black feminist voice in America that would first dare to assert there existed a Black patriarchy, and then challenge the assumptions of that patriarchy by redefining the struggle for civil rights in not just racial terms but also gender ones. They struck the first modern blow for Black women's liberation by their own bold declarations of independent thinking.

It was the independent Black woman, in fact, who became a hallmark of the eighties. She married later, if at all; if she chose to have children, it might have been without a husband. She had a profession, not just a skill; and worked at a career, not just a job. She earned her own money, called her own shots, and expanded the traditional definitions of family values.

Her "family" during the last twenty-five years has just as likely been a sisterhood of close women friends as a clan united by blood and birth. The friendships that have historically sustained Black women became paramount during an era that saw blood relatives increasingly separated by geographical distance while traditional roles between Black men and women came under perpetual fire and conflict.

What distinguishes the relationships between today's Black women is the sheer variety of the girlfriend gatherings. Women still come together in sisterhood in

Actress, singer, and mother, Sheryl Lee Ralph with her beloved son, Etienne Maurice.
December 1993
Photo, Kip Meyer

church and sororities, over coffee in the morning, or drinks after work. But they may also have purchased a car or home together, been the coach for a girlfriend's natural childbirth, started a women's investment club or a breast cancer survivors' group.

Options will perhaps be the century's closing byword, and for Black women options have most often been exercised in the area of personal relationships. Not surprisingly, this extends to the spiritual relationship Black women have developed with their chosen God, for in an era marked by questions, change, and conflict, there is an inevitable quest for answers, stability, and peace.

The quest has taken many paths, been blazed by many guides. And during the past twenty-five years Black women have never been more diverse in the spiritual routes they have chosen to follow or the spirit guides they have chosen to call God. They may pray to Jesus, or now bow to Allah, or chant to Buddha, or pour libation to Shango. Whether they call themselves Christian or Muslim or Buddhist or Yoruba, Black women have remained strong in the faith and found new answers to the challenges of a new era.

If the emotional turbulence that characterized the closing of the century led more Black women to explore and often find solace in "new-age" religions, we also witnessed during this era more visible Black women practicing that old-time religion, Christian ministry. Women such as the Rev. Johnnie Colemon, head of Chicago's Christ Universal Temple, the largest nondenominational church in the country, the Rev. Barbara Harris, the first female to be named a Bishop in the Episcopalian church in 1989, and Dr. Barbara King, an Essence Award-winner and head of one of the largest churches in Atlanta, became popular spiritual leaders in positions that had once been the sole province of men. And some Black women, like journalist Barbara Reynolds, were called to the ministry after many years spent in another profession. Reynolds, the sub-

Elaine Brown, the first woman to head the Black Panther Party, tells her story in A Taste of Power.
June 1989
Photo, Bill Doggett

Jacqueline Jackson, wife of Jesse Jackson, with son Yusef, was dedicated to both the movement and motherhood.
December 1971
Photo, Lou Draper

A tender touch from the first issue of Essence *in the article entitled, "Black Man, Do You Love Me?" May 1970 Photo, Hugh Bell*

ject of an *Essence* lifestyle profile in 1993, returned to school for a degree in theology in 1991 while working full time as a columnist for *USA Today*. And like other Black women who reflect the rich dynamic of our changing lifestyles, Reynolds and her son share a house with six relatives and extended family members.

It is the Black woman's relationship with the Black man, however, that has continued to fuel the passions of our time during this last quarter century. Prophetically, in its very first issue twenty-five years ago, *Essence* raised the question that would haunt us for a generation when it published the article "Black Man, Do You Love Me?" The fact that there has never been a simple answer to this profound question is perhaps at the root of what has been called the "crisis" in Black male-female relationships.

Much of the so-called crisis, to be sure, has been hyped and exploited by the media, which often treats gender conflicts between Black men and women as if they were personal failings and not the common skirmishes inevitable in any war between the sexes. Yet certain Black relationships were to play out on the world stage in the closing decades of the twentieth century that would become a lightning rod for larger issues, forcing both a Black and White public to confront some uncomfortable truths, beginning with the vulnerability of Black male-female interactions.

It was the riveting face-off between Anita Hill and Clarence Thomas during Senate hearings to confirm Thomas's appointment to the U.S. Supreme Court in

When law professor Anita Hill spoke up about sexual harassment, the whole nation listened.
March 1992
Photo, Matthew Jordan Smith

1991 that rocked our sensibilities. We watched, captivated, as a young, poised Black woman became a symbol for an issue as old as women's history in America: sexual harassment. Anita Hill was to do for the evil of sexual harassment what Marian Anderson did for the scourge of race discrimination when she was barred from performing in Constitution Hall in 1939: shame a nation into confronting its own pathologies.

Yet even as new forces threw Black relationships into new conflict, we never lost our flair for romance, our capacity to love deeply, or our enormous style in coming together in committed relationships. Take, for instance, sports commentator Ahmad Rashad proposing to actress Phylicia Ayers Allen on national television during an NFL game in 1985, or Al Joyner joyously embracing and sweeping into his arms Florence Griffith Joyner, his wife and the woman he coached to victory, when she won three gold medals in the 1988 Olympics. Has there been anything to equal such magic moments for the kind of romantic style that makes an entire nation smile?

There has also been the deep and abiding love of Ruby Dee and Ossie Davis to remind us that a marriage can successfully combine passion and political commitment and last over forty years. And there has been the eternal flame of love lost too soon burning in the hearts of loved ones left behind. Two of our best-

Winnie and Nelson Mandela in their Soweto home, only five days after the future president was released following 27 years of imprisonment.
June 1990
Photo, Peter Magubane

Talking, touching, sharing, and caring.
February 1982
Photo, Coreen Simpson

known widows, Coretta Scott King and Myrlie Evers, spent much of the twenty-five years following the deaths of their husbands working to insure that the lives of the men they loved would not go unremembered, nor their murders unpunished. It was Coretta King who worked tirelessly raising money to build The Martin Luther King Jr. Center for Nonviolent Social Change that was founded in Atlanta in 1968, and lobbied to get Dr. King's birthday declared a national holiday in 1986. It was Myrlie Evers who stayed on the case until the killer of her husband, Medgar Evers, was convicted more than thirty years later.

If through the fire and through the storm, relationships between Black men and women have become sometimes torn and battered, they have also proven to be remarkably resilient and, after all is said and done, still loving in the face of great odds.

I think personal transformations need a context. It's not possible simply to dwell on individual attitudes or personal problems outside the context of what's happening to the community, the country, the world. The most effective context in which to bring about changes in the attitudes of men and women toward one another is a context of struggle. As far as relationships are concerned, a lot of historical "mess" has to be gotten out of the way—the sex-based socialization that both men and women have experienced, the confusion that often develops in Black women's lives because we don't realize that we're trying to live up to notions of womanhood that actually have nothing to do with our own historical experience. I think you need both a political and a personal dimension, and when those two can be meshed, then the possibilities of bringing about change will be far greater.

—Angela Davis, "Talking Tough" by Cheryll Y. Greene, August 1986

Black Women have been strong, resilient, hardworking, and determined to overcome formidable odds everyday. The strength of the Black family and the community's rich heritage, spiritually rooted values, and faith have helped us through the challenges and will carry us through the crisis facing our children and families today.

Black children, our children, face the worse crisis since slavery. As Black women we have been bought and beaten, but we have never been broken. In fact, Black women are the cornerstone of the Black family and one of the most important teachers our children have. Today, we have a crucial role to play to ensure that the Black community leaves no child behind and ensures every child a healthy start, a head start, a fair start, a safe start, and a spiritual start in life.

As we have throughout history, we can triumph over poverty, violence, guns, gangs, and too early pregnancy to improve our communities for our children. We must take it upon ourselves to listen, communicate, and educate not just our children but also our communities about the dangers of drugs and guns. We must become informed and involved with legislation that impacts our children and communities. We must stop our nation from imprisoning rather than educating and empowering our young. Together, strong families, strong communities, and most important, strong faith in God can ensure that all children have the opportunity to be their best.

—Marian Wright Edelman, August 1994

TOP ROW:

Daughters of the revolution: Reverend Jesse and Jacqueline Jackson's daughters, Jacqueline and Santita.
May 1986
Photos, Bill Wylie

MIDDLE ROW:

Dr. Martin Luther King, Jr., and Coretta Scott King's daughters, Bernice and Yolanda.
May 1986
Photo, Bill Wylie

Susan Robeson, the granddaughter of activist-actor-scholar Paul Robeson.
May 1986
Photo, Bill Wylie

BOTTOM ROW:

Thandeka, Mpho, and Naomi, daughters of Bishop Desmond and Leah Tutu.
May 1986
Photos, Bill Wylie

Malaak, Ilyasah, Qubilah, and Attallah, daughters of Malcolm X and Dr. Betty Shabazz.
May 1986
Photo, Bill Wylie

If I had to sum it up, I would say that I had a holistic life with Malcolm—the kind of life that one reads about, plans for or wishes for between a man and a woman. I don't think anyone really understood him, the way I understood him. I also think I was destined to be with Malcolm. And I think that Malcolm probably needed me more than I needed him—to support his life's mission. But I don't think that what I would look for in a man today would be what I looked for in a man then. I was very accepting, I just wanted love. I found a sharing and mature man—and I was lucky.

—Betty Shabazz, "Loving and Losing Malcolm" by Susan L. Taylor and Audrey Edwards, February 1992

The tradition of generational love.
April 1990
Photo, John Pinderhughes

Personally I am rather old-fashioned when it comes to who should be the guiding force in the family. I would rather sit back and encourage my man to go forward. I was forced into a role I had no real desire for, and that was to have a career. I was a wife and mother who, unlike the Women's Lib advocates, thoroughly enjoyed it. I enjoyed taking care of my home, my children. I enjoyed sharing his life with him, working along with him. But he was taken from me. I was forced into the role of being head of the household, of having to carve out a career for myself so that my family could survive. I was placed in the same position as thousands of Black women. What do you do when you find yourself in that sort of position? You either fall down or stand up. I tried to face my new responsibility as best I could, and it had nothing to do with Women's Liberation. If I could turn the clock back and place my destiny and that of my children in the hands of Medgar, God knows I would.

—Myrlie Evers, "Conversation" by Ida Lewis, November 1970

OPPOSITE:

Nina Simone with daughter Lisa, uncompromising love.
December 1970
Photo, Kourken Pakchanian

TOP ROW:

Nikki Giovanni, mother of Thomas, then 11.
August 1981
Photo, John Pinderhughes

Shari Belafonte with the first man in her life, her father, Harry.
August 1983
Photo, Francesco Scavullo

MIDDLE ROW:

Young and in love, singer Lenny Kravitz and actress Lisa Bonet.
February 1990
Photo, T. Westenberger/ Sygma

Actors Kadeem Hardison and Jasmine Guy, off-screen.
February 1991
Photo, David Roth

Whitney Houston and Bobby Brown make sweet music in their personal life.
February 1994
Photo, Timothy White

OPPOSITE:

In tune: mind, body, and spirit.
May 1992
Photo, Charles Pizarello

I've also learned that behind the mask of "I know it all" often hide the world's most terrified fools—at least one terrified fool I know personally. With professional help, I came to understand clearly that it's not only me. That most of us operate under the assumption that we must know everything even in situations of change and transition: on a new job, learning a new craft, going to a new country. We believe we can't make a mistake. To question fills us with anxiety. But in real life, people either learn by their mistakes or incorporate them as a way of life.

—Doris Jean Austin, "Holistic Healing," May 1992

Roberta Flack in repose.
February 1989
Photo, Carol Ford

I really think that people should return to some of the things that have made us strong for these many years. If we hadn't been a strong people, we would have crumbled long ago. I don't know which guy was singing "only the strong survive" but it is very true, you know. I think it's time to return to some of these things. Like people ashamed of singing spirituals and all of these things like the Church—it's been a part of our lives. So why not be a part of what's sustained you for all these years and kept you going? That's the reason I tell young people don't write off God. If something is wrong with the Church, stand up and change it and make it be relevant to the community.

—Fannie Lou Hamer, "Fannie Lou Hamer Speaks Out," October 1971

As strange and as difficult as they are, as supposedly backward as they are, they have an astonishing sense of history. They know that until a people, an oppressed people, have actually wrested power from their oppressors they cannot really come into their own. The Bournehills people refuse the many stopgap measures offered to them because, in their minds, the change necessary is a revolutionary change. They will not accept anything less than the complete independence their hero, Cuffe Ned, demanded in his time. Making it on their own. It's the kind of thing that the Cambodians are doing today. Move all the goddamn people out of the cities. Go back to the land. Learn to feed yourself. Be your own people out of the cities. Own your soul. Close the door to the West, like China did for years. Close the West out until you're strong enough to deal with them on an equal level. That's why the Bournehills people are so stubborn and far seeing. They are absorbed and obsessed with the past. They know what history is about; they know what revolution is about.

—Paule Marshall, reprinted from *The Chosen Place, A Timeless People*, May 1979

My religion is my guide to everyday living. I've never wavered in my faith. Never. It's the foundation upon which all else has been built. I think there is movement back to God in our country and I'm glad of that. I think there is also the beginnings of a movement back to the family and that I think is good because my family has been my other strength. I'll never forget the two years spent on tour with my father. I loved his preaching, the hymns he'd sing after the sermon for which I'd accompany him on the piano. I loved his honesty, his sincerity. I remember, as though it were yesterday, his vocal ability and his style, that special talent of his to make things plain. I would be pleased to have my singing described as such. His way was very much my way, and still is.

—Aretha Franklin, "Aretha—Through The Eyes of Love" by Alan Ebert, December 1973

I think ultimately it's a question of focus—of understanding who I am, and of you understanding who you are and what we're each here to do. We will falter unless we know our purpose clearly. My purpose is to do my show every day and to raise the consciousness of my people. My aim is to help people come to know themselves better as I get to know myself better. I am also convinced that the difference between how I handle my life and how some other people handle theirs is that I don't just pray. I truly heed the response I am given. My friend Maya Angelou told me a while back that she thought one of my greatest assets is my ability to be obedient to the voice of God within me, and I think she's right. Losing the weight was a big part of starting that process. Now I can really feel the wind beneath my wings and I'm ready to fly!

—Oprah Winfrey, "Wind Beneath My Wings," June 1989

In addition to her celebrated role in The Color Purple, *Oprah Winfrey has become a force behind the camera and a generous supporter of social causes. October 1986 Photo, Bill Wylie*

Acknowledgments

This book would not have been possible without the great generosity of the photographers and the dedication of the *Essence* team.

Organizing twenty-five years of photographs was a formidable task, accomplished by the tireless efforts of consummate professionals Patricia Black and Robin Taylor. Grateful thanks to Debbie Egan-Chin, Marlowe Goodson, Natalee Huey, Janice Thomas Wheeler, LaVon Leak-Wilks, and Nancy Jung of the *Essence* art department.

An abundance of talents and skills came together in a collaborative effort to produce this book. Special thanks to Marlene Connor, literary agent, and Joan Sandler, style consultant, both whose titles do not reflect the extent of their contributions. Much appreciation to Derrayle Barnes, Simone Dunbar, Karinn Glover, Karen Halliburton, Corliss Hill, Pamela Johnson, Angela Kinamore, Sandra Martin, Stephanie Stokes Oliver, Tara Roberts, Linda Villarosa, Diane Weathers, Valerie Wilson Wesley, and Jamillah Wright.

Special thanks to Harry Dedyo, Sally Elliot, Jim Forsythe, Bill Knight, Elaine Williams, and Suzanne Warshavsky. Thanks also to Regina Barrier, Roger Blondell, Gregory Boyea, Debra Parker, Constance Reid, and Larry Ramo.

At Abrams, special appreciation to Ruth Peltason and Judith Michael.

Endpaper: Top row, left to right: May 1970, photo, Tomas; November 1972, photo, Si Chi Ko; June 1974, photo, Manual Gonzalez; May 1975, photo, Ken Mori; April 1979, photo, Anthony Barboza; September 1979, photo, Rolf Bruderer

Middle row, left to right: February 1987, photo, Dwight Carter; May 1980, photo, Anthony Barboza; June 1988, photo, Buckmaster; September 1989, photo, Dwight Carter; October 1979, photo, Ted Hardin; April 1990, photo, Todd Gray

Bottom row, left to right: May 1991, photo, Charles Bush; February 1988, photo, Dwight Carter; February 1992, photo, Lawrence Henry Collection, Schomburg Center For Research In Black Culture, The New York Public Library, Astor, Lenox, and Tilden Foundations; July 1993, photo, Nicola Dill; December 1993, photo, Kip Meyer; January 1994, photo, Matthew Jordan Smith